Strategic Acceleration

*The belief that greatness already exists
becomes the enemy of mastery.*

—Tony Jeary

Praise for Strategic Acceleration

"*Strategic Acceleration*, by author and CEO coach Tony Jeary, presents a methodology to keep those who want to win focused and on message to efficiently execute relevant, high-leverage activities that create results—faster."

—*Consulting Magazine*

"I've known Tony for years, and his ability to build great leaders, great thinkers, is extraordinary. *Strategic Acceleration* will help you cultivate an attitude of willingness, embrace change, clarify your vision and focus, and deliver results. The advantages you gain can change the trajectory of your life."

—Stephen M. R. Covey, *New York Times* bestselling author of *The Speed of Trust*

"Over the years I have learned that it takes both a certain mind set as well as living by real success principles to achieve great things. Let Tony Jeary share his insights with you."

—Ken Blanchard, co-author of *The One Minute Manager*

"This book will impact the way you think about results and the way you go about achieving them."

—Zig Ziglar, *New York Times* bestselling author of *See You at the Top*

"What Tony shares in *Strategic Acceleration* about clarity, focus and execution is extremely valuable for anyone want to excel."

—*SUCCESS Magazine*

"Whether you are in sales or are the CEO of a billion-dollar corporation, let Tony Jeary be your personal coach."

—Mark Victor Hansen, *New York Times* bestselling author of *Chicken Soup for the Soul*

"This book gives you powerful tools and techniques for thinking and action that will enable you to get more done, faster and easier than you ever thought possible."

—Brian Tracy, author of *No Excuses!*

Strategic
Acceleration
Succeed at the Speed of Life

Tony Jeary

A Member of the Perseus Books Group

Published by Vanguard Press
A Member of the Perseus Books Group
First paperback edition 2010

Designed by Joseph Parenteau
Set in 12-point Sabon

Library of Congress Cataloging-in-Publication Data

Jeary, Tony, 1961–
  Strategic acceleration : succeed at the speed of life / Tony Jeary
    p. cm.
  HC ISBN 978-1-59315-501-8 (alk. paper)
  PB ISBN 978-1-59315-564-3
  1. Success. 2. Change (Psychology) 3. Self-management (Psychology) 4. Self-
actualization (P)sychology) i. Title. ᐟII. Title: Succeed at the speed of life.
  BF637.S8J43 2009
  650.1—dc22
                                                          2008039342

Vanguard Press books are available at special discounts for bulk purchases in the
U.S. by corporations, institutions, and other organizations. For more information,
please contact the Special Markets Department at the Perseus Books Group, 2300
Chestnut Street, Suite 200, Philadelphia, PA 19103, or call (800) 810-4145, ext.
5000, or e-mail special.markets@perseusbooks.com.

10 9 8 7 6 5 4 3 2 1

CONTENTS

- Without Clarity, You Will Resist Strategic Change
- Perception Is Reality, Even if It's Not the Truth
- The Things You Believe Impact Your Results
- The Value of Changing Strategic Beliefs: A Case Study
- Strategic vs. Tactical
- A Lack of Clarity Creates Felt Needs
- You Can Live in the Problem, or You Can Live in the Solution
- Increasing Effectiveness Is the Strategic Issue in Improving Results
- The Effectiveness Ladder
- How Far in the Future Can You See?

- A Clear Vision Is Critical to Success and Effectiveness
- The Value of Combining Opportunity with Personal Strengths: A Case Study
- Vision Can Transform the Worst of Circumstances
- Getting Better, Not Bitter: A Case Study
- Get Clear on What You Really Want

- Focus
- Getting Clear on Current Conditions
- Strategically Merging Positives and Negatives: A Case Study
- Venturing Into the Gap
- Strategies, Objectives, and Action Steps
- Putting Value in Perspective at The News Group: A Case Study
- Organizing Your Goals and Locating Your Focus at Three Levels
- Differentiating Your Focus at Each Tier of Your Vision
- Putting It All Together

- The Strategic Acceleration Tripod
- The Execution Tripod
- Persuasion Is Critical to Execution
- What It Means to Exceed Expectations
- How Exceeding Expectations Impacts Results
- Understanding Expectations
- Persuasion Is the Key to Exceeding Expectations
- The Three Elements of Effective Persuasion

- The Procrastination Problem
- Identifying the Foundations of Procrastination
- Procrastination Is Just a Bad Habit!
- Go as Far as You Can See, and Then You'll See Farther

- Your "Strategic Presence" Defines Other People's Perception of You
- The Building Blocks of Strategic Presence
- Your Values Contribute to Your Strategic Presence
- Your Behavior Also Contributes to Your Strategic Presence
- How to Communicate Strategically

- Creating Images of Influence
- Your Vision Statement
- Your Behavioral Priorities
- Presence Statements and Characteristics
- Why These Building Blocks Are Important
- Creating and Sustaining a Positive Strategic Presence Requires Repetition

  - Exercise 1: Create Voluntary Change
  - Exercise 2: Understand Your Influences
  - Exercise 3: Understand Your Strategic Beliefs
  - Exercise 4: Outline What You Need to Do to Get What You Want
  - Exercise 5: Document Your Vision
  - Exercise 6: Unlock Your Internal Keys to Success
  - Exercise 7: Explore Where You Are Today, Why You Might Not Be Going Where You Want, and What Can Be Changed
  - Exercise 8: Document Your Vision's Purpose and Value
  - Exercise 9: Create Your Own Recipe for Clarity

  - Exercise 10: Evaluate Your Current Focus Skills
  - Exercise 11: Improve Your Focus Skills
  - Exercise 12: Get Clear on Current Conditions
  - Exercise 13: Develop Your Strategic Plan

  - Exercise 14: Determine What to Say and How to Say It
  - Exercise 15: Give Value and Do More than Is Expected
  - Exercise 16: Document What Is and Is Not Working Well

A NOTE FROM TONY JEARY

When the original manuscript of Strategic Acceleration was completed, the world was different from the one we live in today. Barack Obama was still merely a candidate for the presidency. The economy was growing. Unemployment was less than 6 percent. By the time Strategic Acceleration was published in March 2009, the pace of life was accelerating. Unemployment was climbing, and the U.S. economy was declining fast.

Now, one year after the hardback edition of Strategic Acceleration appeared, this trade paperback edition is being released. The world continues to change, and the pace of life has not decreased; if anything, it has increased. Unemployment is above 10 percent. The federal deficit is skyrocketing. Millions of small business owners are terrified of the economic challenges ahead of them, and large corporations are trying to discern appropriate strategies to take them forward. The future appears very murky.

The incredible change in the United States and in the world since *Strategic Acceleration* was first conceived has proven that people need to understand how to cope with the speed of life. The principles in this book outline a way to achieve that understanding, and concentrate on three core issues: clarity, focus, and execution. These principles will provide sustenance and hope to any person or business trying to determine what to do next.

If you are caught up in the turmoil of change and uncertainty but are committed to winning in today's world, you desperately need to read this book and do what it suggests. If you take this advice, I promise three things:

1. Your fear or concern about the future will be greatly reduced.
2. You will be more confident and will have more control over your life and your business.
3. You will have a solid strategy to help you get better results, faster, while living in harmony with rapid change and with the speed of life.

Sincerely,

Tony Jeary

FOREWORD

In 1994 Zig Ziglar and I were flying from Dallas to Detroit for the purpose of meeting with executives of the Chrysler Corporation. I was the CEO of Zig's company at the time. The year before, we had entered into an agreement with Peter Lowe Seminars for Peter to be Zig's exclusive seminar sponsor for public appearances. The audiences Peter was able to attract for Zig numbered 15,000–20,000 people. Our strategy in creating those events was to broaden Zig's recognition and exposure in corporate America. Our visit to Chrysler was one of the first fruits of that strategy.

As our aircraft winged toward Detroit, a young man came to our seats, knelt down in the aisle and introduced himself. That young man was Tony Jeary. He told Zig how important Zig's books and tapes had been to him and what a pleasure it was finally to meet him. This was not an unusual event, because Zig is frequently recognized as he travels. But there was something about Tony that set him apart for me. The guy seemed to be much more than a fan. He was serious, and he was focused!

After some initial pleasantries, we shared that we were on our way to visit Chrysler Corporation and were going to be submitting a training proposal to them at some point in the future. That's when I got my first exposure to the Tony Jeary who would occupy a significant space in my life for the next 15 years! Tony told us that Chrysler was one of his largest customers and began to ask us all kinds of questions about the people we were talking to. It became evident that Tony had the entire Chrysler organization chart in his head and understood their internal politics and how they made decisions. The following week, I called Tony and hired him to help us create our Chrysler proposal!

In 1996 I left the Ziglar organization and returned to my independent consulting practice. Tony had become a relatively close associate of mine by then, and to my surprise he became my customer when he hired me to help him create a revised strategic plan for his career. After we completed that project, I continued to coach him periodically from the sidelines for the next ten years. I watched him stay faithfully focused and execute his vision and his plan. His client base broadened, and he became the coach to many of the world's top CEOs and hundreds of successful entrepreneurs and business owners. He was having a huge impact on his customer's success and becoming incredibly successful himself.

During the ten-plus years that I coached Tony from the outside, we had periodic conversations about possibly joining forces and working together on a full-time basis. However, we could never seem to find enough compelling reasons to take that step, so nothing progressed in that direction until 2006. In the spring of 2006 Tony and I were discussing some things, and I said, "You know, I think we need to really figure out why all these great people are coming to you and better understand the real value they are getting from you. I have a suspicion they are getting a lot more than communication strategy." We decided that I would conduct some lengthy, personal interviews with thirty of Tony's best long-term customers. What I discovered in those interviews was amazing to me, and it eventually led to the book you now hold in your hand.

What I discovered in those interviews also convinced me to finally join with Tony on a full-time basis and become the

President of his company. I remember Tony asking me why after ten years I was willing to throw in with him completely. I said, "It's simple: These interviews demonstrate that you have the opportunity to really impact people in a powerful way and accelerate their results. You have what it takes to accomplish something that is very significant, and I want to be a part of that! This is something I can really get excited about."

What did we discover in the interviews of our customers? The interviews kept producing the same three words over and over again: Clarity–Focus–Execution! Tony was helping people get clarity for their strategic vision, helping them focus on the things that really matter and to develop powerful strategies to execute their vision. As a result, his customers were able to improve their results significantly within time frames that they had not believed possible. This was consistent across the board with all of them!

All through 2007 we continued to analyze and dissect the critical factors that enabled our customers to get superior results faster, and we named this new methodology Strategic Acceleration. Strategic Acceleration is about speed and results, and we suspected this was something a lot of people would need and want. To test the water with our new approach we created a small passport-sized booklet called "Passport to Strategic Acceleration" and mailed out about 5,000 copies to various people, businesses, and organizations. Immediately the phone started ringing, and one of the calls came from the office of the Sergeant of Arms of the United States Senate. The Sergeant of Arms is like the CEO of the Senate and manages an organization of several thousand people. The Senate hired Tony to address their top leadership group of 150 people and to share the Strategic Acceleration methodology. This confirmed we had something to offer that was significant and valuable.

During my business career which has now spanned over three decades, there have been several questions that have been constants in my mind. What is the greatest single factor in success and achievement? What is it that really separates good from great, and great from mastery? What is it that ignites a vision that can't be stopped? I believe this book provides powerful answers to these questions. I believe the book you now hold in your hand can become one of the most powerful tools you will ever have, if you let it speak to you and if you will do what it suggests. So, read on and let Tony Jeary lead you through the powerful principles and concepts that will produce Strategic Acceleration for your business and your life!

The book you have in your hands is the foundation for it all.

> Enjoy, learn, and I wish you the best
> Jim Norman, President
> Tony Jeary International

ACKNOWLEDGMENTS

I am blessed with a fantastic team of people who have helped me over the years, both with my clients and with this book.

Thanks to Jim Norman, who is our company president, as well as my adviser and friend. He invested almost two years in researching and helping me craft, write, and organize this methodology, which is based on the work we've done together over the past decade and a half.

Thanks to our chief marketing officer, Sara Keech, who has traveled tens of thousands of miles working alongside me and helping me help hundreds of clients. She has a special gift and talent for words, and patience for the sometimes-crazy collaborative process I use. Her efforts really rounded out the chapters to make them clear and inspiring for readers of any age, experience level, or professional focus.

Thanks also to my publishing team. Peter Miller, my literary agent, connected my works to the right people. Roger Cooper, my publisher, really understands how to work with focused experts like myself and how to help us share our messages with the world. And Ruth Mills, my editor, brought her years of wordsmithing expertise to us to ensure the book was organized and valuable. Finally, thanks to Joe McNeely at Brilliance Audio who enthusiastically agreed to publish the audio version of this book.

I am so grateful to others on my team who helped shape, organize, and move this methodology (taught to top achievers in my Strategic Acceleration Studio) into the core manuscript.

Thanks so much to my intrepid office manager, Eloise Warden; my indefatigable personal assistant, Adrienne Williams; my longtime business manager, Tawnya Austin; my literary adviser, Tammy Nolan; and my personal coach for over twenty years, Mark Pantak.

George Burke, Nonie Jobe, Ross Lightle, and George Lowe all kindly reviewed the book and offered keen insight that helped make the final manuscript strong and genuine. And of course many others contributed in different indirect ways. I appreciate all of you!

I know this methodology will help hundreds of thousands succeed in this busy, fast-paced world. Much success!

Strategic
Acceleration

INTRODUCTION

This book provides a simple, strategic thought process that will transform the way you think, live, and work. It will forever change the way you think about getting results and will increase your effectiveness in all you do. By the time you finish this book, you will be able to achieve a higher level of clarity about what you really want; you will understand how to focus on high-leverage activities that accelerate the results you seek; and you will be more prepared to confidently execute your dreams or vision.

Let's face it—the speed of life today is hectic and fast-paced. Time is the most important capital you have, and most people feel overdrawn. You do not seem to have enough time to nurture all your priorities—which might include mentoring others, spending time with people who are important to you, innovating and dreaming, and learning and growing. Even when you define priorities and set out on a plan to reach a new level of success, personal availability always seems to shrink. Priorities get pushed aside by noisier demands for your personal time and energy. Superiors, peers, and team members may require more from you. You may be side-tracked by departmental overhauls or market changes. Others' problems may become your own through convenience or proximity. Before you know it, your predefined priorities are just a vague idea and you're moving farther and farther away from what you initially set out to accomplish.

People are frustrated by the challenges of getting more done faster and not having a methodology or process that will allow them to make it happen. There is no shortage of high-tech tools to help you. Productivity software, faster computers, and lots of new gadgets are constantly advancing in ways designed to help you—at least in theory—simplify your life and your work. We all live in the midst of the search for the holy grail of technology: one device that will do it all! We sense the possibility of an ultimate solution if we can get our cell phones, our Internet, our appointments, our task lists, our projects, and indeed our entire life neatly packaged in one handheld device. We sense that when this is achieved, our lives will become more manageable, efficient, and successful. Unfortunately, this is not going to happen.

"*It's not the big that eat the small—
it's the fast that eat the slow.***"**
—Jason Jennings

I am a firm believer in utilizing technology to its fullest extent, and I don't believe any of us can maximize our success without it. However, something is bubbling beneath the surface of the high-tech waters that intuitively warns us that technology is not the primary issue when it comes to results. Have you ever heard someone who achieved great success give credit to his iPhone or her BlackBerry? Do we ever hear athletes on championship teams give credit to their productivity software or their new, faster PC for the trophy they have won?

My approach to understanding what it takes to be successful is to see the entire matter as a results contest. Successful people get superior results, faster! Unsuccessful people don't!

Superior results depend on knowing how to get them, and knowing how is characterized by putting all the pieces together that allow execution of a vision. Succeeding at the speed of life requires that you get superior results, faster, and that you do it on purpose.

❝My approach to understanding what it takes to be successful is to see the entire matter as a results contest. Successful people get superior results, faster! Unsuccessful people don't!❞

If you ask ten people to define success, you will get a variety of answers. Some will say you are successful when you are happy. Some will say success is achieved when you have acquired a certain amount of money or a list of "things." Some relate success to certain specific achievements in their personal or business life. All of those are legitimate descriptions of success. The point is that success is a moving target for many people, and it has to be more specific. One of the questions I frequently ask people is, *"What does success mean to you?"* This question always triggers a great conversation, and through the years, I have distilled a simple definition that most people seem to agree with:

We are successful when we
achieve objectives we have
established in advance.

Anything else is by chance or serendipity. The most successful people live their lives on purpose. They don't sit around waiting to see what might happen next. They know what they want, and they are clear and focused about how they will achieve it.

If you are an entrepreneur pursuing a vision, this book will illuminate and expand your thinking about what you need to do to execute that vision in the most powerful, effective way possible. If you are a senior executive of an organization and seek an effective strategy to elevate your team's effectiveness, *Strategic Acceleration* will show you a simple, commonsense method to make that happen. If you are a team leader and seek an effective way to coach and inspire your team members to higher levels of performance, *Strategic Acceleration* will help you do that. If you are an individual who wants to accelerate your personal success and break out of the status quo by learning how to consistently exceed expectations, *Strategic Acceleration* is your passport to a higher level of success.

I have more than eighteen thousand contacts in my Rolodex, carefully collected and nurtured over the past twenty-five years. They are friends as well as clients who have sought my coaching, training, and strategic collaboration services. I have worked closely with and mentored thousands of them. Leaders of some of the largest corporations and organizations in the world (a short list includes Wal-Mart, Samsung, Ford, Sam's Club, Qualcomm, New York Life, Firestone, and even the U.S. Senate) seek my strategic coaching expertise. Many others are successful entrepreneurs, some of whom appear on the *Forbes* list of the world's 400 wealthiest people. These results-focused high achievers often come to work with me in my Strategic Acceleration Studio—a custom-designed, high-tech facility that combines the latest media technology with a library containing a lifetime's worth of systems, processes, and best practices. I have spent the past quarter century helping successful people become more successful.

In 2006, my business was booming, and I wanted to fully understand why so many successful people sought my coaching services, the initial basis of which was communication strategy, and why they continued to retain me as a long-term strategic partner and guide. I wanted to understand the real nature of the value I was providing to my clients so I could document, study, and replicate it even better for others.

The president of my company conducted lengthy, independent, and personal interviews with thirty of our best long-term customers. We asked them how I had helped them reach greater success (which we defined as achieving objectives established *in advance* and *on purpose*). After synthesizing all of the responses, we discovered that we were consistently providing our clients with the ability to significantly accelerate their results within time frames they had not believed possible. Through the proprietary processes I facilitated during our strategic coaching sessions, I helped them develop:

- **Clarity:** the ability to get clear about what they really wanted to achieve
- **Focus:** the ability to avoid distractions to concentrate on high-leverage activities that produce the most significant results
- **Execution:** the ability to use strategic communication to exceed expectations and get results faster

Clarity, focus, and execution are the three basic components of *Strategic Acceleration*, and all successful people and organizations have them in common. The eight chapters of this book detail those components, using real-world examples from people of all professions and walks of life to help you understand. Each of the chapters closes with Very Important Points to help you zero in on the most critical information and retain it more efficiently. And Appendices A, B, and C will guide you through a series of exercises designed to help you define and document how you'll achieve superior results faster.

What I've learned through the years is that most people can become successful high achievers when they get their *why* and *how* questions answered. That is really what the *Strategic Acceleration* mind-set will consistently produce. When you have clarity concerning your vision, then focus becomes possible. When you are focused, the ability to execute is achieved, and results are the ultimate fruit of a well-executed vision. Great execution flows from a great design, and great design is deployed through strategic communication. You will have all of those things by the time you finish reading this book, so let's get started. Turn the page to accelerate your success and succeed at the speed of life!

CHAPTER 1

The Speed of Life and What You Believe

☛ *You need to cultivate an attitude of willingness to help you better navigate the choppy waters of change.*

There has never been a time when opportunity and technology have come together so perfectly. The competitive playing field has been leveled to the extent that a small business or even an individual can compete and win at almost any level. Large companies are able to powerfully niche their brands and touch their markets in ways never thought possible in times past. You can access information in an instant and you have access to tools and resources your not-so-distant ancestors would have considered to be items from a science-fiction novel.

"The speed of life" is a term you intuitively understand the moment you hear it. It paints a picture of fast-paced living and a glut of opportunities and choices that require constant decisions. It is a term that carries the optimism of opportunity, and it is a term that imparts a sense of stress. Whether you consider it positive or negative, the speed of life is a time-gobbling reality and you grapple with it from the time you wake up until you go to bed at night. For employers and managers the speed of life might mean living in a fishbowl of litigation, regulation, criticism, and competition. For employees the speed of life may mean coping with policy changes, financial adjustments, and ever-increasing workloads. For husbands and wives the speed of life may involve dealing with distractions that erode communication and trust and create relationship problems. For parents of a growing family it might represent a nonstop treadmill of activity that requires juggling schedules for sports, dance and art lessons, and birthday parties. For children the speed of life requires them to live in the powerful grip of peer pressure that asks them to grow up faster than they should. The speed of life is tough, it is real, and it impacts you at every juncture of life.

Though the speed of life has some challenges, it also provides incredible benefits. You live in the most exciting, prosperous time in the history of mankind. The world population now approaches seven billion people. That means there are lots of people who have plenty of ideas, and all of them want something! That provides an incredible base of human creativity and ingenuity. Information and technology are bringing the world together rapidly and have produced an unprecedented period of innovation and advancement in just a few generations. The past fifty years in particular have contained a mind-boggling amount of human progress, and there appears to be no end in sight. Personally, I love living in this age. I can get more done, faster, and have a wider range of choices and activity than ever before. There is no greater time to live than today, but never before has there been so much fast-paced pressure.

Chances are, you live on both sides of the speed of life: You have some stress, and you also have lots of benefits. In the years ahead, our most significant personal and professional challenges will be learning how to live and succeed at the speed of life and to be content with it.

The speed of life is not new, because people have always believed that life demanded more from them than their time allowed. That's why time-management solutions have always been popular. In fact, the first product to improve time management may have been the wheel! However, in every era, some businesses always manage to do better than others, and at a personal level, some individuals always are more successful than others. Successful businesses and successful people have had one characteristic in common in every age. That same characteristic also provides a powerful distinction that separates those who succeed from those who don't. What is the characteristic? It is this:

> Successful businesses and successful
> people know what they really want
> and are willing to do whatever it
> takes, within the parameters of
> integrity and honor, to get it.

When thinking about the speed of life and its effect, you could place businesses and people in two categories: Those who have *clarity* about what they want, and those who don't. The speed of life affects these two groups in completely different ways. Those who have clarity about what they want do not feel as stressed or rushed by the speed of life. They are able to approach each new day knowing what they need to do, and they go after it with energy and eagerness. They have a clear vision and are focused on their opportunities. They know how to execute their strategies to get the results they want. Organizations and people with clarity do not have to be goaded or pushed into effectiveness; instead, they are pulled toward their vision with amazing power. If you know what you really want, the opportunities and choices you have will be more abundant and you will have greater confidence in your efforts. If you do not have clarity about what you want, the speed of life will become a time-gobbling reality and you will struggle with it from the time you wake up until you go to bed at night.

❝*Those who have clarity about what they want do not feel as stressed or rushed by the speed of life.***❞**

To succeed at the speed of life, you must be clear and focused on the *high-leverage activities* that are most relevant to your strategic agenda. What is relevant to your success and achievement, and what isn't? The activities and strategies that capture your time and attention should be those that most directly impact the results you need and want, right? Therefore, the ability to identify and focus on your most significant, high-leverage activities is the major factor in improving and accelerating results. Being clear about what you really want empowers you to make those strategic choices better!

The speed of life has not changed the basic fundamentals of achievement; it has merely reduced the amount of time you have to do what you need to do. In years past, when the speed of life was slower and change was less dynamic, planning could take place at a more comfortable pace. This is no longer the case. Planning today must almost be done on the fly to meet competitive challenges. In many instances, businesses face scenarios that demand almost *simultaneous* planning and execution. For example, fuel costs in 2008 skyrocketed in a few short months, which forced some businesses to go back to the drawing board to create survival strategies. The fuel costs particularly impacted commercial airline companies and trucking firms. As they made new plans, they had to implement them almost simultaneously.

Without Clarity, You Will Resist Strategic Change

Strategic change demands a lot of emotional energy because it requires new thinking, which in turn disrupts *comfort zones*. We all know how people resist leaving their comfort zones! That is why change is a big deal to people and is so difficult to achieve at an organizational level. The pain that accompanies change can be financial, physical, or emotional, but regardless of the type of discomfort created by change, the speed of life demands that you embrace it if you intend to be competitive and effective.

Admittedly, change is not a simple subject, but there is a simple fact about change that is undeniable: Unless you are willing to change, you won't. This means that the *willingness* to change plays a huge role in your ability to succeed. I'm talking about *voluntary change*, which does not require anyone to push you or mandate that you do new things. Common sense dictates that the difference between change being traumatic or reasonably acceptable is directly related to the *willingness to change*. Voluntary change is proactive, and it can't wait to get started. If you are an employer or a manager, you need a strategy that will produce voluntary change in specific people as well as across the organization. At a personal level, you need a strategy that will produce voluntary change in yourself. Appendix A includes an exercise called a Change Audit (see Exercise 1), which will help you develop this strategy and increase your effectiveness.

Perception Is Reality, Even if It's Not the Truth

Though the speed of life creates circumstances that are very real, its pressure is caused as much by perception and feeling as by fact. The way you *feel* about these pressures is a direct re-sult of what you *believe* about your opportunities and the choices you make daily. As you live your life, you are con-stantly making value judgments, forming opinions, interpreting events, and making decisions about what you will and will not do. With respect to the results you get, the decisions you make about what you will or will not do are the most significant.

**"*The thing always happens that
you really believe in, and the belief
in a thing makes it happen.*"**
—Frank Lloyd Wright

We all have a way in which we view the world, our role in that world, and the relationships we have with everybody in it. Called the *belief window*, it contains everything you be-lieve to be true, false, correct, incorrect, appropriate, inappro-priate, possible, and impossible. Two things are happening in your belief window:

1. It is framing all of your views of people, places, and things, and creating the perceptions and feelings you have about everything.
2. It is influencing the actions you take regarding those same people, places, and things.

Your belief window determines all of your choices and ac-tions, and it allows information you consider important to enter your mind and be retained. It also blocks out what you do not consider important and screens information and circumstances you don't think you need. *If you aren't aware of what you need, however, you will not recognize the importance of things that might be critical to your success.* Your belief window could cause you to block certain pieces of information from further consideration, and you may miss some great opportunities as a result. That is why you must be very clear about what you really want and what you really need to achieve it. Exercise 2 in Appendix A will walk you through describing your belief window, which will clarify how you see the world and help you discover how that outlook affects all choices and decisions.

The Things You Believe Impact Your Results

It takes great effort and discipline for personal success, and your belief window determines how effectively you are able to perform because it ultimately controls all of your choices and actions. Our belief window is shaped by the facts or ideas we accept as truth and our personal experience as it relates to those facts. The speed of life presents a constant, unending flow of information that contains a mixture of fact, truth, myth, rumor, and in some cases downright deception.

❝Our belief window is shaped by the facts or ideas we accept as truth and our personal experience as it relates to those facts.❞

Your belief window doesn't always provide a wholly accurate view, however. This potentially results in significant errors in the way your mind filters the information that passes through it. What are the consequences of your belief window framing something incorrectly? What if your belief window causes you to take action or inaction based on something that just isn't true? How would this erroneous framing of an event, an idea, or a person impact your results? If your error in perception involves a significant principle necessary for achievement, it might stop you from taking an important step toward success, or it might even cause you to fail completely. Therefore, you need to have the ability to adjust your belief window when it impedes your success.

You started forming your belief window from the very first moment you began to interpret your surroundings. You were very young when you began this process, and you will continue to make adjustments to it for the rest of your life. As you grow older, however, you become less willing to adjust your belief window. The saying that it's hard to "teach an old dog new tricks" is true. As you mature, you finalize and fill in most of the foundational strategic principles you will accept in your life, and when that strategic framework is complete, those principles will dominate everything else in your belief window. It is extremely difficult to add anything new to your belief window that conflicts with one or more of your strategic principles, but there are instances when both should be altered to be more successful.

The Value of Changing Strategic Beliefs: A Case Study

One of my clients is a perfect example of how results can be accelerated by changing strategic beliefs. George Burke is a very successful entrepreneur who owns a relatively large commercial paint-contracting business in Atlanta, Georgia. His client list includes Target, Emory University, Georgia State University, Kaiser Permanente, and Days Inn, among others.

When I first met him several years ago, he was already successful by any standard you could apply. George had a great family and a great business, and he made a great living. George was very happy with his life and work, but he felt "maxed out" with respect to future opportunity. He had built his company around himself, and he believed he had to be personally involved in a long list of responsibilities to maintain its success. And because the things he did personally ate up all of his time, he believed he was out of options for future growth.

George did not believe he could go beyond where he was. He had a self-limiting belief about himself and his business. He believed he had hit the ceiling of success for his business and that was just the way it was. His self-limiting belief was that his growth potential was directly related to the availability of his personal time. He erroneously believed that he was the sole person capable of both selling and managing major projects, which was an enormous drain on his time and energy.

In working with George, I was able to help him replace that strategic belief with another idea. The new idea was that it was possible for him to duplicate himself in others by finding and training individuals he trusted, individuals who would sell and manage important contracts with just as much care and concern as he did personally. In the next eighteen months, George told me he duplicated himself four times in others, and the result has been that his business revenues doubled! This duplication freed up his time and permitted him to concentrate on new opportunities and think more strategically. His success grew exponentially simply because of changing one strategic belief.

Strategic vs. Tactical

The word "strategic" deals with "why" issues, whereas the word "tactical" deals with "how." Your belief window (the "why" behind your actions and choices) is therefore a set of strategic beliefs. When your strategic "why" beliefs become muddled, your tactical "how" solutions diminish. When your strategic "why" issues are settled, the tactical "how" solutions become obvious. Therefore, the degree of clarity you have about your strategic beliefs enables you to focus and execute.

The speed of life is a 24/7 frontal assault on your belief window, and it causes confusion due to the sheer volume of information that confronts you daily. You can't possibly test or experience all the information that assaults you. Trying to get your mind around more than you can process puts you at risk of being distracted from the things you need to do that really matter. The speed of life confuses the way you view your future because you become unclear about what you believe the future has in store for you.

As a result, you are at risk to buy into self-limiting beliefs about what you can or should do. Achieving clarity about what you really want is the solution because knowing what you want helps settle and establish the strategic issues you face. If you are not clear about what you really want, however, your belief in your effort will not be powerful or compelling enough to sustain your efforts. Clarity about what you want is actually what empowers your ability to believe in what you are doing, because your belief in what you are doing is the engine of the actions you take.

A Lack of Clarity Creates Felt Needs

Over time, the speed of life creates a mixed bag of erroneous strategic beliefs that combine to produce a list of specific felt needs. *Felt needs* are the emotions we feel as a result of unresolved questions and challenges. What are those felt needs? There are many, but I believe that essentially two are the most significant. Each of them can be traced to a lack of clarity.

Here is a brief discussion of each and why they are caused by a lack of clarity:

1. "There is not enough time to do all I have to do": Anything worth doing should be done—period! When something is worth doing, there are always options available to get it done. For example, I recently met with a CEO client of a billion-dollar company who wanted to develop a new program that would add value for the company's corporate customers. The idea involved his company doing some things it had never done before, and the CEO's perception was that everyone was too busy to take on the new project. He said they just didn't have enough human bandwidth to get it done.

I told the CEO that the problem might not be a lack of bandwidth; instead, the real problem was a probable lack of clarity regarding how the idea would work and what the details of the program would require. The problem seemed like a human bandwidth issue because of the time and effort it would take to turn the strategy into an effective process his people could execute comfortably. His perception (belief) was that it would take too much time for his people to work out the bugs and become effective.

That his people were busy and had packed calendars was a reality, and the feeling of not having enough time was legitimate. However, the problem was not a time problem; it was a clarity deficiency. I pointed out that the new project could be farmed out to a third party to execute and work out the bugs and gain the clarity they needed to make the program work. Then, when the correct model was factually known and understood, it could be handed off to his people, and they would be able to quickly become effective. This solution required the CEO to change a strategic belief. Again, the problem was not a lack of human bandwidth it was a lack of clarity.

2. "The results I am experiencing are less than I want or expect": It is only when you begin to do things differently that your results will begin to change and improve. Only a small percentage of the things you do are high-leverage activities that can significantly move the results needle. Superior results come from the ability to focus daily on high-leverage activities that have the power to make a real difference. Clarity enables you to identify those high-leverage activities and remain focused on them. For example, after my friend George Burke duplicated himself in others, he suddenly discovered lots of additional time that allowed him to focus on the high-leverage activities, which allowed him to double his revenues in eighteen months.

▪ ▪ ▪

If you relate to the above conditions, it's a fair assumption that you need to adjust one or more of your strategic beliefs. This is a polite way of saying that you need to develop a new way of thinking about what it takes to really be successful in your professional and personal life. You believe some things to be true that are not, and the probable cause is a lack of clarity. George Burke believed he had reached the ceiling of success for his business, which was not true. He had no clarity about how to break through that ceiling, but he wanted to. Fortunately, he had the most important ingredient: *willingness!* All George needed was clarity to make it happen.

Do you agree that you may have some things in your belief window you believe to be true that aren't? If you don't think that statement is accurate, I want to challenge you with this little exercise. Take a piece of paper and travel back in your mind about ten years. Try to make a short list of some things you believed ten years ago that you no longer believe. For example:

- Have you changed your spiritual beliefs?
- Have you changed your political persuasion?
- Have you made changes in value judgments about certain people?

You should be able to come up with several things for your list. What are the chances that ten years from today you will be able to do the same exercise and get the same results? I'd say it's somewhere in the vicinity of 100 percent! This means you have things in your belief window *today* that you will reject as false over the next ten years. This little exercise demonstrates that there is a high probability that you currently believe some things to be true that aren't true—you just haven't yet acquired enough new information that will allow you to change your opinions. However, until you willingly let go of your false beliefs, they will limit all that you do. Exercise 3 in Appendix A takes you through this process via a strategic belief adjustment, which will help you determine what influences you need to change to relieve subsequent limitations.

Your problem and mine is that we are in a state of not knowing what we believe to be true that is not true. Right now, we think that everything we believe is true. The only way to purge our incorrect beliefs is to expose them—and we need to adopt a process that will help us expose them. Becoming clear about what you really want is a huge step in that direction.

You Can Live in the Problem, or You Can Live in the Solution

The challenges that accompany the speed of life are real, but there are far more opportunities than problems. Every day you make a choice about your attitude, which is shaped by your belief window. If you believe life is just a big pile of problems, you will be less than optimistic about the future. On the other hand, if you believe life is just a nonstop joy ride of unending bliss, you are going to get a rude awakening when real problems darken your door. The truth is that life is a combination of problems and blessings, and you are going to experience both from time to time. A far better view of life recognizes both conditions but is committed to the importance of living in solutions rather than problems.

"*If you choose to live in solutions, the world eagerly awaits your dreams and provides every tool and opportunity you need to turn them into reality.***"**

When I conduct strategy sessions with my clients and we begin the process of building clarity, there is frequently a mind-set that has to be overcome about living in the problems. For some reason, the human mind naturally seems to gravitate to all the reasons that something *can't* be done. It happens over and over again, and it is caused by a belief window that makes it difficult to think in terms of solutions. When someone casts a vision for something new, the knee-jerk response is to immediately think of all the reasons it won't work. The focus is totally on living in the problems and obstacles that will block doing the new thing. When you are not clear about what you really want, your natural tendency will be to emphasize problems rather than solutions.

If you choose to live in solutions, the world eagerly awaits your dreams and provides every tool and opportunity you need to turn them into reality. However, if you choose to live in problems, you will see little opportunity. This is where clarity can make such a huge difference in results. When you lack clarity about what you really want, you will find yourself being pushed toward living in problems. When you have clarity about what you really want, you will be pulled toward living in solutions. Living in solutions allows you to become more effective in all you do.

Increasing Effectiveness Is the Strategic Issue in Improving Results

Increasing your effectiveness always requires change, which is why I've devoted much of this chapter to the subject. As I said at the beginning of this chapter, change is difficult because it makes you uncomfortable. Change makes you uncomfortable because it asks you to do unfamiliar things. But increasing your effectiveness requires change, and you will not achieve optimal effectiveness until you are once again comfortable with actually doing the new thing. A lot has to happen between your ears for new activities to become comfortable, and you have to master new attitudes, new tools, and new skills as well.

> **"**Communication is a skill that you can learn. It's like riding a bicycle or typing. If you're willing to work at it, you can rapidly improve the quality of every part of your life.**"**
> —Brian Tracy

In every new endeavor, you must take four specific steps before you will become effective. Think of it as an *Effectiveness Ladder* with four rungs. Each rung has its own characteristics and contains an action milestone you must complete. The Effectiveness Ladder is important because climbing it takes time, and until you reach the fourth rung, you will not be comfortable with what you are attempting to do. The speed of life demands that you be able to climb this ladder much faster than in years past.

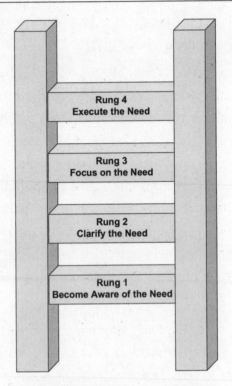

The Effectiveness Ladder

Rung #1: Become Aware of the Need

The speed of life is introducing new technology and information at lightning speed, and much of it you don't even know about. It is only when you become aware of something that you can recognize a new need. Before you have this awareness, you don't even know that you don't know! This is the rung you have to climb before you can undertake anything new.

For example, if you had never seen or heard of global navigation systems, you would not even be aware that you didn't know anything about them. You would have no awareness of them and would not even realize they might be of practical value to you.

Rung # 2: Clarify the Need

On this rung of the Effectiveness Ladder, you become aware of what you did not know. However, you still can't do whatever it is you did not know. Using the global navigation system example, this rung would mean that you are now aware of what such a system can do and that it could be important to you, but you still wouldn't know how to use one if your life depended on it. It is in this stage that you make a decision to either move forward and learn how to do the thing you didn't know about, or just ignore it and walk away. So clarifying your need is critical, and the speed of life presents many potential needs.

Rung # 3: Focus on the Need

On this rung of the ladder, you will embrace the need you have discovered, and you will begin to take action to respond to it. This is the rung on the ladder where your time investment begins in all you do. This rung of the ladder requires you to learn and change. It's not easy in the beginning.

In the case of using a global navigation system, it could mean that you have browsed the manual and have explored its basic operation, but you still have to think carefully about everything you do. You may have to keep the manual nearby and refer to it continually, or be constantly fumbling around with using the system. However, you remain focused on your effort because you understand the eventual benefit of your time investment.

Rung #4: Execute the Need

As you climb this rung of the ladder, the action you take to accomplish the task in question becomes second nature to you, and you are able to execute and deploy the skills you have learned with effectiveness. The key here is that effectiveness and skill make you comfortable with the subject or activity. You know your subject and have practiced long enough to do it with minimal thought or effort. At this point, you have become effective with the new concept, skill, or tool.

Continuing with the global navigation system illustration, you now can turn it on and effortlessly use it. It has become a powerful tool in your life and you don't have to think about using it.

▪ ▪ ▪

How does the Effectiveness Ladder relate to the speed of life? The speed of life is constantly adding to the list of things you know little or nothing about. As a result, there are more new things to become aware of, but becoming aware can be a time-consuming process that is not productive. Succeeding at the speed of life demands that you keep up with innovation, products, concepts, and tools that can make you more effective, but you can't chase after every new thing that comes down the road. The reality is that there is more information out there than you can reasonably process.

The foundational solution to this challenge is to have clarity about what you really want. If you don't have clarity about what you really want, you will not be able to make good choices about where and how to invest your time. Every new thing you want to master will require you to climb the Effectiveness Ladder. To succeed at the speed of life, you must find a way to expedite change and to climb the Effectiveness

Ladder more quickly. The ability to do all these things is powered by *clarity*, engaged with *focus*, and converted into superior results via *execution*. All three of these components must be in place, and if one or more is absent, your results will not meet or exceed expectations.

How Far in the Future Can You See?

A major premise embedded in Strategic Acceleration is to go as far as you can see, and then you can see farther. I know you remember when it was reasonable to consider your plans and strategies on a five-year basis. A traditional question you have heard many times is "Where do you want to be in five years?" That question is now somewhat obsolete because of the speed of life. A more relevant question today is "Where do you want to be next week?" That's a bit extreme, but that's what it feels like sometimes. You can plan only as far as you can see. That is the point.

For example, during my work with George Burke, I asked him what he thought about clarity and how his understanding of clarity had changed. Based on his own experience, George said he thinks everyone has things in their belief window that limit what they believe they can accomplish. When George achieved the limit of what he thought he could do, there was a feeling of "now what?" that settled over his life— and when that happened, he lost clarity. He believes his own lack of clarity became evident when he reached whatever success ceiling he had imposed on himself by his own beliefs. Therefore, to maintain clarity it demanded that he purge those self-imposed beliefs regularly. I certainly agree with George, and Strategic Acceleration optimally requires an annual purging, at a minimum.

George also told me he feels he gained clarity when he had a perfect blueprint of what he needed to do and accomplish for the next twelve months. This blueprint, which I helped George create, enabled him to predict exactly where his business would be at the end of the twelve months. To create that kind of blueprint, you have to think deeply about all you do and why you do it. Then you have to transition the results of your thinking into action to gain new experience. New experience is required to be able to see farther, which is also what you have to do to climb the Effectiveness Ladder.

A Clarity Blueprint includes the following key components:

- *What* you want to do
- *Why* you want to do it
- *How* you will do it
- The *benefit* of doing it
- And the *negative result* of not doing it

When you know all these things, you will achieve clarity and you will be clear about what you really want. I'll show you how to create your own Clarity Blueprint in Appendix A, Exercise 4.

The speed of life limits to about one year the length of time your Clarity Blueprint can be effective. In the course of that year, many things will change that you could not have predicted and over which you have no control. For example, any Clarity Blueprint created on January 1, 2007, that depended on fuel, transportation, or travel for its success was in jeopardy by January 1, 2008, purely because of skyrocketing energy costs. Such is the nature of the speed of life, and that is why clarity requires an annual adjustment of your thinking.

When an artist prepares to carve a new sculpture, he or she starts with a block of wood, stone, or clay. A successful artist knows exactly what is hidden within that block and systematically begins to remove all the material that conceals the image that only the artist can see so clearly. When the chipping away of excess material is complete, the result is a piece of art that matches the image the artist visualized from the beginning. The key to an artist's success is the clarity the artist has about what he or she wants the finished work to be. Artists are clear in their minds about what they want and expect.

In the same way, if you want to succeed at the speed of life, you must have clarity about what you really want.

Summary

The speed of life demands that you embrace change and work within it. This means that the *willingness to change* plays a big part in your ability to succeed both personally and professionally at the speed of life. If the results you've been getting have not been what you expect and want, you need to become willing to *change the way you think,* so you can change what you have been doing and influence change in others. If you are a leader, you need a strategy that will produce voluntary change in your organizations and in specific people. At a personal level, you need a strategy that will produce voluntary change in yourself!

The next chapter deals with a crucial component of that strategy: developing an authentic vision. Not only does an authentic vision provide the power to produce that necessary voluntary change, it will motivate and set benchmarks for your success.

Very Important Points

▶ Unless you are willing to change, you won't! This means that the willingness to change plays a huge role in your ability to succeed. What I'm talking about is voluntary change, which does not require anyone to push you or mandate that you do new things. Common sense dictates that the difference between change being traumatic or reasonably acceptable is directly related to the willingness to change.

▶ You make all decisions based on your personal belief window, which frames all your views of people, places, and things and influences the action you take regarding those same people, places, and things. Some of these beliefs may be erroneous, and Strategic Acceleration is the process to expose and purge them.

▶ If you feel there is not enough time to do all you have to do or that the results you are experiencing are less than you want or expect, you probably need to make some adjustments in one or more of your strategic beliefs. This is a polite way of saying that you need to develop a new way of thinking about what it takes to really be successful in your personal and professional life.

CHAPTER 2

The Pulling Power of Clarity: Vision

☞ *An authentic vision motivates, provides the power to change your behavior, and sets benchmarks for success.*

In Chapter 1, we discussed the need to develop a willingness to change, which is critical to keeping up with the speed of life. In today's highly competitive world, however, success hinges on more than simply keeping up—successful people get *superior results,* which rely on having a strong vision.

As a professional person, you probably wear many hats. Some of them cover your work and professional life; some cover your role as a spouse or parent or pertain to family; and some cover the time you invest in community service through your place of worship or other benevolent organizations. Although the hats you wear differ, your time and effort are invested in *anticipation of getting certain results.* The nature and the specifics of the anticipated results may change, but every activity has a results payoff—be it good or bad. The point is that the processes that produce superior results in your business life are no different than the processes that produce results in your private life. Success is success, and results are results. The principles of Strategic Acceleration are applicable to every activity you undertake. These principles involve:

1. Clarity
2. Focus
3. Execution

This chapter deals with *getting clarity about your vision*—the first step toward Strategic Acceleration. The real issue is success and getting superior results, which always begins with a vision.

❝The real issue is success and getting superior results, which always begins with a vision.❞

The epitome of producing success and achievement is to discover the basis for creating the kind of human desire that causes voluntary change. *Voluntary change* is the ultimate goal that every leader hopes to instill in others, and voluntary change is the key for you to break out of whatever conditions exist in your business or personal life that may be holding you back. My experience is that when you really have the "want-to" factor, you will find a way to do whatever it takes to get what you want. This opens the discussion of vision and why it has the power to create desire and the willingness to change. Bluntly stated, *vision has the power to transform your behavior like nothing else!* Vision is the elusive ingredient that will consistently produce "want-to," and ultimately it leads to voluntary change.

You need to get your mind around a basic truth about change: Greater success and superior results always require personal change. The reason is obvious:

> If you keep doing the same things
> over and over again, you will
> keep getting the same results.

This statement has become a pop definition of insanity, but it's also the way most people live their lives. An unwillingness to change is more of a symptom of commitment to the comfort of current conditions than a reflection of insanity.

Regardless of what prevents it, change is difficult, and the fact is that you do things the way you do them because you believe that's the best way to do them. After all, your actions are just the fruit of things you believe (as I pointed out in Chapter 1). This fundamental fact is the reason acquiring a vision is so powerful. Until you acquire a vision powerful enough to impact the things you believe, your behavior is unlikely to change. You will be content to remain in existing conditions and keep doing what you have always done. If you make that choice, you will continue to get the same results. This is easy to understand but difficult to implement.

If you are a business owner or manager in a corporation, you are very familiar with the difficulty of creating voluntary change in your employees and associates. The reason for the difficulty is that people resist climbing the Effectiveness Ladder (discussed in Chapter 1) when it comes to doing something differently. People know that climbing the Effectiveness Ladder will disrupt their comfort zone, and it will take time to regain that comfort. Comfort zones are called *comfort zones* because they can be *comfortable!* The only thing required to remain in a comfort zone is to close yourself off to new ideas and refuse to change. Over the years, I've learned that nothing very interesting or innovative ever emerges from a comfort zone, except more plans to make the comfortable *more* comfortable.

Comfort zones impact all of us. When people in organizations become too comfortable, it's because they have lost the momentum to pursue their vision. Why? Because they've accepted where they are as the best they need to be or do.

> **❝A** *vision not only becomes something to* motivate *you and to provide* the power to change your behavior, *it also becomes the plumb line or* measuring stick *that helps you keep everything together as you execute your plans.***❞**

So what's the problem? The problem is that people who are comfortable and content aren't going to do anything new. Comfort zones are a huge drain on organizational energy, which is the collective sum of the human spark that powers the desire to win, produces creativity, supports persistence, and establishes the foundation for organizational commitment. When organizational energy is degraded or lost, all of these qualities begin to diminish and the ability to achieve superior results becomes less likely. When organizational energy is reduced, it produces a group of people wandering around in their comfort zones who resist change at every turn. The leadership solution is to create and communicate a powerful vision that will reverse the lethargy and reignite the desire to win and do more than expected.

A Clear Vision Is Critical to Success and Effectiveness

It is easy to understand why vision is a critical element in success, when you understand what success really is. Here is my definition of success:

> We are successful when we achieve
> objectives we have established in advance.

If you have no vision, there is nothing to tie your objectives to and nothing to help you measure your performance or progress. So a vision not only becomes something to *motivate* you and to provide *the power to change your behavior*, it also becomes the plumb line or *measuring stick* that helps you keep everything together as you execute your plans. This all works well when you have a clear vision, but what do you do if a clear vision for the future has eluded you? In Appendix A, Exercise 5 can help you develop your vision so you can plan for your success.

The Value of Combining Opportunity with Personal Strengths: A Case Study

During the mid-1990s, I was traveling more than twenty days each month. I had multiple offices in the United States and in the Far East. I was working around the clock, compensating for jet lag and time zones. This was a time in my career that I was being pulled in many directions, and I was pursuing every opportunity that presented itself. I was achieving a lot financially, but I wasn't living a life congruent with my personal values. I did not want to be an absentee father and husband—and that is exactly what I was becoming.

It occurred to me that the vision I had for myself was not as clear as it needed to be. I had a fairly clear concept of what

I wanted to achieve, but I had not established a clear picture in my own mind of what I really wanted overall in my life. It was at that point that I decided to apply to my own life the principles I teach others. That meant creating a new vision by getting clarity on what I really wanted.

"*People who produce good results feel good about themselves.*"
—Ken Blanchard

As I began to evaluate my situation, I could see that I had created many objectives and goals for myself, but they were objectives that were created in response to short-term opportunities. For example, if Chrysler Corporation (a major client for me in the 1990s) asked me to create car dealership strategies for Japan, Taiwan, Korea, and China, my response was to open an office in those countries. That is how I wound up paying rent all over the world. Somehow I had to find a way to reconcile and bridge my opportunities with a strategic vision for my life.

I began this process by looking at all the opportunities before me. I separated them into two groups:

1. The first group involved opportunities to do things I was excited about.
2. The second group involved opportunities that would require more of my time than I was willing to give.

After creating my opportunity inventory, I took an inventory of my greatest strengths and weaknesses. I identified the things I really loved to do and the things my customers seemed to value most about the work I did for them. When I married the opportunity inventory to my strengths, a very clear picture of what I wanted began to form. I wanted to become a strategic coach to top business leaders and entrepreneurs. I also wanted a minimum of travel, I wanted to create value in the lives of my customers they would find nowhere else, and I wanted them to rave about me to others so I could continue to grow my client base.

As soon as that vision became clear in my mind, I discovered I was being pulled forward in the most powerful way I had ever experienced. I immediately started doing things that would allow me to turn that vision into reality. Within two years, I had closed all my satellite offices, built a high-tech Strategic Acceleration Studio on my estate in Dallas, and begun hosting strategy sessions for my customers in this special facility.

This brief synopsis of my journey to clarity and vision illustrates the practical steps in creating my vision. Simply stated:

> Vision is created by combining opportunity with your personal strengths and talents.

I changed my vision to capitalize on what I really loved to do, what I knew I was good at doing, and what was best for my family. I eliminated or reduced actions that took away time or energy from the things that improved my life and increased my happiness. I looked for new opportunities that better suited my personal strengths and talents, and I was able to realize increased satisfaction and success as a result.

Vision creation (and modification) requires that you engage your brain in focused thinking about your opportunities. The human mind is an amazing machine, but too often we attempt to get it to do things beyond its design. The brain does a lot of things, but its primary, conscious function is to reason and reach conclusions. It is in the process of thinking and reasoning and reaching conclusions that the brain produces what we call ideas. Where we get off track is when we think our brains are capable of developing completely new ideas. The brain can't do that! Your brain just puts things together that may not seem to be related and creates *new possibilities* out of those connections.

Another way of looking at this process is to say that when your brain makes creative connections, it has the power to recognize new opportunities. Those opportunities come in the form of ideas. It is the recognition of opportunity that allows you to birth and launch a vision.

We've all heard the saying "opportunity knocks," but when you understand how your brain works, you can easily see that opportunity does not knock. Opportunity simply exists if the right connections can be made concerning some facts. These facts just need something to connect them and turn them into new possibilities. So if you feel that opportunity has passed you by or that you have not had many opportunities, it's probably not true. Instead, *you just haven't connected the events in your life with something you really want*. When you can make that connection, opportunities will suddenly appear everywhere.

Vision Can Transform the Worst of Circumstances

It is a fact of life that people are not born on an equal playing field. Some begin their lives in better circumstances than others, and they had little to do with those circumstances: Their parents and ancestors get that credit. It is a reality of human existence. Some would say people who are born into great poverty or other circumstances have zero opportunity

and no hope. But that idea is not correct! Far too many people have escaped horrible conditions on the back of a powerful vision, because an authentic vision has the power to *pull*
people out of their circumstances and pull them toward a better life.

To illustrate this truth, I want to share a story with you
about a man named Albert Mensah. It is a simple story, but
it powerfully demonstrates how the dynamics of a clear vision
can produce incredible change in a life.

Getting Better, Not Bitter: A Case Study

Albert was born in a mud hut in the African nation of Ghana.
The poverty he lived in is so foreign to the American experience that it is difficult to even imagine. When he was six years
old and physically able, Albert was given work that involved
making two trips a day to haul water more than two miles
from distant wells to his home. His family needed this water
so they could drink and bathe.

When Albert was ten years old, the circumstances of his
life changed a bit: His father obtained a job with the government and his family moved to the capital city. The move did
not mean Albert's family had become rich; it meant just that
they had escaped the mud hut. Even in their new home, Albert's family still lived at a poverty level far below the worst
conditions you might find in America.

One day, Albert's father took him to see his first movie. It
was an American movie, shown in a barren warehouse, and
the movie screen was a bedsheet. The thing that struck Albert
about the movie was that everyone in the movie was wearing
shoes. This may seem like a small thing to Americans, but to
Albert, it was a life-changing revelation. He had never owned
a pair of shoes, and from the moment he saw that movie, a vision formed in his mind about going to America. He wanted

to go live in the place where everyone had shoes! The "want-to" factor had been created in Albert Mensah, and it changed his life.

Albert's vision of going to America was something he talked about all the time to his friends. The response he got was ridicule and teasing. They even went so far as to nickname him "States" because he constantly talked about going to America. The nickname was intended to be a condescending joke. Nevertheless, from the age of ten, Albert embraced his vision, and he committed his mind to discover a way to America.

When Albert was twelve, it was time to decide where he should go to high school. There were two Catholic schools in his city, but one of them, St. John's, had more American teachers and more books. Albert's family encouraged him to attend St. John's because of his dream to go to America. They reasoned that if he could find a way to go to St. John's, the American teachers might help him find his way to the United States. Albert was accepted as a student at St. John's, and it was there that he discovered the library and the power of books. He learned that by reading books, he could travel anywhere in his mind and learn anything he needed to learn.

Albert also learned about the existence of pen pals. There were people in America to whom he could write and from whom he could learn more about America. Upon this discovery, Albert began a relentless pen-pal writing career. He corresponded with scores of Americans and other people all over the world throughout his high school years. He asked them lots of questions, and one thing he discovered was that American universities would frequently offer scholarships to foreigners like him, if they qualified.

To make a long story short, after applying to and being rejected by more than three hundred American colleges and universities, he eventually received a full scholarship from Western Maryland College near Baltimore.

Albert came to America at the age of eighteen, and he graduated from Western Maryland College four years later. Upon graduation, he was ready to step out and pursue the American dream. Unfortunately, Albert could not get a job equal to his education level. His American dream turned into washing dishes in a Marriott hotel. He and his new American wife scratched out a meager existence living in a small attic apartment. Equal opportunity still had a way to go in the United States, and Albert experienced discrimination about being black and being from Africa. However, Albert's response was to get better, not bitter. He had come too far to be held back by a little discrimination.

Albert's response to his circumstances was to set a goal of becoming the best dishwasher the Marriott Corporation had ever seen! His stellar dishwashing performance and work ethic eventually led him to a promotion: He became a "bar back" in a Marriott cocktail lounge, cleaning up after the bartender and keeping the bar stocked with supplies. The pay wasn't much better than when he had been a dishwasher, but it did put him in contact with the public. Albert noticed that lots of people came into the lounge who appeared to be financially well off. These people said they were in sales. Albert didn't know what being "in sales" meant, but he was willing to try it if it might get him out of Marriott's kitchens and cocktail lounges.

Albert got a job selling yellow-pages advertisements, and he became one of the company's top five salespeople in the United States. When he started selling yellow-pages ads, he knew nothing about selling. So on his first day, he found out the name of the most successful salesperson in his office. Albert made friends with that person and asked him what he needed to do to be successful. He got the information and copied that behavior. Within a year, Albert was the top salesperson in that office.

Albert also became an avid consumer of sales training products and attended many seminars conducted by sales experts and motivational speakers. Watching these people conduct their seminars sparked a new vision for Albert: He wanted to become a professional speaker and conduct his own seminars. He thought he had a lot to say about opportunity and success and that people would like to hear him talk about it.

Albert joined Toastmasters, and during his first year of membership, he won second place in Toastmasters' worldwide speaking competition. This positioned him to begin his own speaking career, and today Albert travels the world sharing his opportunity message more than a hundred times every year.

He has also created a financial foundation to help poor children in Ghana, and he travels back to his home country twice each year to build on that effort. He is supported in that project by the government and the president of Ghana himself.

Not bad for a poor African boy who began life with no hope, no skills, and what many would say was a life doomed to poverty because of no real opportunities!

Get Clear on What You Really Want

What I love about Albert Mensah's story is that it engages several powerful principles, and it illustrates the *pulling power* that comes from being clear about what you really want. For most of us, going to a movie is probably not sufficient to produce a powerful lifelong vision. However, in Albert's case, that is exactly what happened. The reason the movie had such a powerful effect on Albert was that he became powerfully clear in his own mind about what he wanted. It wasn't complicated: He wanted to come to America so he could have shoes. *Why* the movie had the effect on Albert is not as important as the *effect* it produced: complete clarity about what he really wanted, and that is the most important piece of the vision-creation puzzle. I call this the *clarity effect*.

❝*Discipline is the bridge between goals and accomplishment.*❞
—Jim Rohn

In Albert's story, we see that he became clear in his mind about what he wanted before he was able to actually do anything to pursue the vision. It was purely the power of the vision that enabled him to take the action steps in subsequent years that eventually led to his college scholarship and a new life in his adopted country. Becoming clear about what he wanted allowed him to discover and attend St. John's school, where he made his first real connections to America. That happened a few years after Albert first saw the movie that sparked his vision.

Upon being accepted by St. John's, Albert discovered the library and the power of reading and education. It was in reading books that Albert discovered the possibilities of becoming a pen pal. From becoming a pen pal, Albert discovered the possibility of receiving a college scholarship from an American college. Albert's relentless persistence in writing to American colleges and universities ultimately led to his scholarship, which became his ticket to America.

Do you see the series of small progressions that led to Albert coming to America? What he did at any given time was to go as far as he could see . . . and then he could see farther.

When Albert first saw the movie and the vision of America became fixed in his mind, he had no opportunities before him that would actually take him to America. He was merely clear in what he wanted, and he had seen opportunity in that movie. Because he was clear in what he wanted, every thought in Albert's mind was constantly engaged to find some meaningful thing he could do that would move him one step closer to his dream. Because of that, Albert was constantly pulled toward the vision. Nobody had to push him. His behavior to do whatever it took was driven by his belief that it was possible for him to make it to America. All the changes he made were voluntary and came as a result of being clear about what he really wanted.

Whatever your vision, Albert is a great example of the value of really believing in what you're pursuing and making voluntary change. Each great journey or success is a series of small steps and manageable tasks, and with the completion of each, more opportunities and paths will become evident and will open up to you. Having true clarity about what you want will pull you toward success.

Recognize the Opportunities in Your Own Life

One of the seemingly miraculous effects of becoming clear on what you want is that you begin to see new opportunity everywhere. When you are not clear about what you want, it may seem that your opportunities are slim or none. Actually, without a clear vision, there probably isn't much opportunity you can identify, because there is very little going on in your head that gives you the ability or the desire to recognize opportunity. When you become clear about what you want, you suddenly begin to see that everything in your life up to that very moment has uniquely prepared you to do the very thing you now see so clearly. You are also able to make the connections between the *daily events* of your life and how they are really *opportunities* that will take you one step closer to your vision.

**❝*You have to be smart.
The easy days are over.*❞**
—Robert Kiyosaki

Do you feel stagnant in your business or in your personal life? Do you feel you have accomplished all you can with what you have? This is where George Burke, the Atlanta entrepreneur described in Chapter 1, found himself: He thought he couldn't be any more successful in his business, yet after he developed a clear vision of what he wanted, he doubled his business revenues in only eighteen months. I would say to you that none of those feelings—of stagnation or complete accomplishment—are actually true. You just need to become clear about what you want, and new opportunities will be certain to appear. The opportunities you discover will come in the form of small, reasonable steps you can take that will move you a little closer each day to turning your vision into reality.

Taking small steps is what all of life is really about, and this action is the true basis of achievement. The mathematical possibilities of winning the lottery are almost incalculable. In the same way, the mathematical possibility of doing one huge thing to achieve a dream is equally remote. You can find isolated examples of overnight success, but for most of us, "overnight success" actually results from taking lots of small steps that are connected to our dream. In Appendix A, you will create an action plan (see Exercise 4) to help you create the steps (tasks) and deadlines to realize your dream.

Docking a Ship Seems Impossible, But It's Actually a Series of Small, Easy Steps

Have you ever been on a Caribbean cruise? When those large cruise ships arrive in the smaller ports, docking the ship is a marvel to behold. On the dock is a large cleat, and somehow the ship's crew must manage to secure a rope from the ship to the cleat. The rope is huge, and it is far too heavy to simply throw to someone standing on the dock.

So the first thing that happens is that someone from the ship throws a small ball of twine to a person standing on the dock. The ball of twine is easy to catch and easy to handle. That ball of twine is connected to a small rope that can also be easily handled, yet is strong enough to haul in a much larger rope, which is the real objective. The big rope is attached to a huge winch onboard the ship. The deckhand on the dock reels in the twine and the small rope and then drags the big rope over to the cleat, where it is easily attached. At that point, the powerful winch on the ship takes up the slack in the big rope and positions the huge ship snugly alongside the dock.

This vividly illustrates how we need to approach opportunity. You may see something really big in your vision, but it may be like the big rope—too big to lift and too heavy to throw. What you need is *a series of smaller connections* that will allow you to better manipulate and manage your larger opportunity. The only thing you have to worry about is whether the opportunities you pursue are really connected to your ultimate vision.

Understanding Your Gifts and Strengths Is Critical

I believe that at some point in life, most people have a dream, but something happens to it over time. Every elementary schoolchild is asked, *"What do you want to be when you grow up?"* If you have ever seen children confronted with this question, you see how quickly they respond, with little hesitation. Some say, "I want to be a fireman." Some say, "I want to be a pilot." Others may say they want to be a doctor or possibly even the president of the United States. Yet very few of these schoolchildren actually live out their childhood dreams.

Did you have a childhood dream you eventually achieved? Most of us don't. As adults, many people still find themselves asking the question, *"What do I want to be when I grow up?"* This leads us to an obvious question we need to answer about ourselves. Was there a time in your life that you had a vision and there was something you really wanted to achieve? My guess is that you would respond *yes*. So what happened to you along the way, if you were unable to execute your vision?

There are two main reasons you might decide to give up on your dreams:

- The first reason is that you aren't clear about what you really want.
- The second reason is that you did not approach your opportunities properly.

You may have believed you had to do things that were big, huge, and significant. What you actually need to do is *connect a series of small steps and opportunities* that will eventually produce the final result you want. Go as far as you can see, and then you will see farther! For Albert Mensah, it was going to the American school, communicating with pen pals, and writing to American colleges in pursuit of a scholarship. What are the opportunities *you* need to connect to turn *your* vision into reality?

Short of seeing a movie that provides a lifetime inspiration, I believe authentic vision of the kind discussed here (you'll create your own in Appendix A, Exercise 5) will be most frequently discovered or birthed from your own personal experiences, strengths, and gifts. Each human being can lay claim to something he or she has that no other person has. And that includes *you*. The unique thing about *you* is *your own life*. The exact experiences you have lived are as unique as your fingerprints or your DNA. Although many lives may exhibit some common experiences and characteristics, the unique experiences of *your* life belong to *you* and *you alone*. Within those unique experiences, your gifts and talents are exposed. In Appendix A, Exercise 6 offers you the opportunity to think through and document what makes you special. This will help you capitalize on your unique strengths.

**❝*Go as far as you can see,
and then you will see farther!*❞**

Each of us has the ability to do a particular thing and to do it very well. For some people, it may be the ability to teach and explain things. For others it might be the ability to wade into complicated situations and discern simple solutions. For others it may be the ability to write. Still others may have the gift and ability to create poetry, music, or another art form. For some it might be mechanical skill or athletic ability. Whatever your gifts or talents may be, they can be seen as an unbroken thread throughout your life. Our talents and gifts become evident when we are young, and they continue to be refined and revealed until we die.

The most significant fact about your gifts and your talents is that they involve things you probably *love* to do. Think about it: Nobody has to *push* you to do those things. You do them because they give you pleasure and because in doing them, you feel you have provided value for others as well as yourself.

For that reason, I believe authentic creation of a vision begins with *embracing your gifts and talents*. I refer specifically to the talents and gifts that allow you to exceed others' expectations. When you recognize and claim your talents within the context of value creation, you will begin to see connections that lead to an authentic vision, with the power to transform your professional and personal life and possibly the lives of many others.

How does all of this work for a business? There is no difference. Organizations have unique skills and abilities because the people who populate the organization have unique skills and abilities. In the same way that personal gifts and skills are seen throughout an individual life, they are also seen in the life of an organization. There are certain things your business does very well, and the ability to do those things differentiates you from your competition. Understanding those advantages is critical to sustaining organizational success and effectiveness over the long haul.

Summary

Achieving clarity of vision is the cornerstone of Strategic Acceleration. When you have an authentic vision, things happen. When you have clarity about your vision, you discover yourself being pulled toward it, and all you have to do is follow the connecting opportunities that carry you along. The *pulling* effect of an authentic vision allows you to make connections faster. You can identify and pursue opportunities faster. The results you achieve will be superior, and they will come faster than you may have thought possible.

Chapter 3 covers the importance of understanding the "why" behind your vision. Having clarity of purpose and vision, as well as the ability to communicate it to others on whom your success relies, will continue to pull you forward.

Very Important Points

▶ Taking small steps is what all of life is really about, and this action is the true basis of achievement. The mathematical possibilities of winning the lottery are almost incalculable. In the same way, the mathematical possibility of doing one huge thing to achieve a dream is equally remote. You can find isolated examples of overnight success, but for most of us, "overnight success" actually results from taking lots of small steps that are connected to our dream.

▶ You are successful when you achieve objectives or goals you have established in advance.

▶ If you have no vision, there is nothing to tie your objectives to and nothing to help you measure your performance or progress. So a vision not only becomes something to *motivate* you and to provide *the power to change your behavior*, but it also becomes the plumb line or *measuring stick* that helps you keep everything together as you execute your plans.

▶ Achieving clarity of vision is the cornerstone of Strategic Acceleration. When you have an authentic vision, things happen. When you have clarity about your vision, you discover yourself being pulled toward it, and all you have to do is follow the connecting opportunities that carry you along. The pulling effect of an authentic vision allows you to make connections faster. You can identify and pursue opportunities faster. The results you achieve will be superior, and they will come faster than you may have thought possible.

CHAPTER 3

Understanding the "Why" Produces Clarity

☞ *You must know why you do what you do, which requires that you understand the purpose and value of all that you do.*

C hapter 2 discussed the importance of having clarity about your vision, which enables you to identify and pursue opportunities more rapidly. But think about that word, *clarity?* What does it really mean? What does it mean to *you?*

To research definitions of the word is an exercise in trying to understand something intangible, critical, and personal. It's a perception, it's a process. Some people describe clarity as a *special focus* that permits them to see, without impediments or biases, what truly matters to them. For others it's an *awakening,* a *revelation,* almost an *epiphany* when it's realized. Still others would say that it's an *uncluttered understanding* about their purpose, their priorities, and their path. All of these definitions are good ones, but we must all have our own unique grasp of what the word means to us.

"Clarity." What a word; what a concept! I spend quite a bit of my time writing, thinking, and teaching others about this dynamic seven-letter word. It's such an important word, full of potential, promise, and possibility, and it holds the destiny of individuals and organizations in its powerful grip. It's something we all should want, seek, and have, right? To really move beyond where you are now and reach the next level of your success, you simply must have clarity. But how do we get it?

> **❝The basic definition of clarity is *having* an unfettered view of your vision, *which is what you want and why you want it, fed by an understanding of its purpose and value.*❞**

As with all complex constructs, there is a starting point upon which subsequent layers of understanding and application will reside. I believe that the first step in obtaining clarity is to agree on a simple definition and build on it from there.

The basic definition of clarity is having *an unfettered view of your vision,* which is what you want and why you want it, fed by an understanding of its purpose and value. To better explain, here is a model of what I call the *Clarity Equation*:

The Clarity Equation

What + Why	
Purpose + Value	= Clarity

The rest of this chapter examines the equation's components and sets you up for developing your own Clarity Equation in Appendix A (see Exercise 9), complete with details and actions.

What & Why: Developing Your Vision & Understanding Your Influences

What + Why	
Purpose + Value	= Clarity

So ask yourself the following:

- What do you *really* want?
- *Why* do you want it?
- What is your overarching objective, the thing you desire the most, and why is it so important to you?

That's your vision. If you can articulate that vision, you've taken the first step toward developing clarity. You've cut the key to your potential! Now it's time to open all the other doors you'll encounter, and quite possibly create, just by having this initial clarity.

I am hoping that the above word "why" really triggered some new thinking for you. We all know what we want, for the most part. But do we all really know why we want it? Sometimes the "why" can make or break us as we reach for success. The "why" deeply influences the actions you take . . . or don't. It's guided by your beliefs, perceptions, and attitudes, all of which develop over a lifetime of experience of sorting out the "why" of other things. In other words, if you don't understand the "why" behind your vision, your belief may not be legitimate or sufficient enough to support your own voluntary change, much less influence others to change. Simply put, you won't fully believe in your vision until you understand the "why" of it.

"*Why*" is clarified by understanding purpose and value. Most important, it relates to the positive perceptions people have about purpose and value. If a small group of people creates a plan that is mandated for others to follow without ensuring those people have a positive perception of the plan, then focus and execution will be bumpy, to say the least. If there is a negative perception of purpose and value, there will be no willingness to exceed expectations or change voluntarily so that superior results can be achieved. Consequently, leaders will have to *push* the team, rather than permit the vision to *pull* people toward it. For this reason, "*why*" becomes the critical issue of perception, and to achieve clarity, it must be addressed.

"*If you're alive, there's a purpose for your life.***"**
—Rick Warren

How many of us have experienced conversations with our children that pursue endless variations of "why" questions during their growing years? Children want to know the "why" of things before they willingly and cheerfully comply with parental instructions. Parents don't always do a good job of dealing with the "why" questions and wind up having to *push* their children into compliance. It seems that children are born with the "why" question burned into their brains, and it surfaces about the time they develop the ability to speak. (A friend of mine jokingly said his daughter's first word was not "Mama," it was "why"!)

The desire to know why doesn't go away when children become adults. They just don't push the issue as aggressively as they did when they were children. However, the issue of "why" remains in the forefront of every human mind, even if the question is not asked. The point I'm making is that just because leadership decides that a certain vision or direction is correct, it does not mean that clarity has been achieved within the context of perception. The purpose of it all, the "why" of things, must be perceived by those who are required to execute the vision. The same principle holds true at a personal level. Just because you decide you need to do something doesn't mean you will do it.

Enabling Transparency: A Case Study

I have a good friend who recently shared a story with me about some things that happened in his church. The church was a relatively small congregation of about forty people. They were as unified as any group of people you might hope to find. The group had existed for almost a decade, and during that period of time, there was no hint of disunity or disagreement about anything. This small church had no debt, a 6,000-square-foot church facility with no mortgage, and $150,000 cash in the bank. The offering plate was never passed, and there were never any open attempts or solicitations to raise money. The members simply gave voluntarily as needs arose, without being pushed. They financially supported a half-dozen missionary families around the world and actively ministered to the needs of their local community as well.

Then the pastor made a personal decision to retire and leave the church. For some reason, he did not believe it was important for anyone to know he was leaving, and he didn't think it was important that the members of the church have any input in the selection of his replacement. The pastor counseled with three church elders, and those four people decided the future fate of the church and made no effort to gather feedback from other church members about anything.

❝*Don't be afraid to see what you see.***❞**
—Ronald Reagan

One Sunday morning, the pastor made an announcement that he was leaving in three weeks, and he named his replacement. The emotional effect on the church was disastrous because of the perceived secrecy that surrounded the entire transition process. There was no clarity because none of the members understood why the transition had been handled in that fashion.

Few major undertakings or changes can be accomplished in a vacuum. True success relies on the support and buy-in of others. You must understand the reasons why your vision is important, and you need to be able to clearly communicate that importance. Just as clarity *pulls* you (and others) forward toward realizing your vision, a muddled message about the "why" will almost certainly ensure that you are *pushed* away from your success.

Purpose: Communicating Motivators

What + Why	= Clarity
Purpose + Value	

What's your purpose in life—do you know? One of the most successful books of this new century is *The Purpose-Driven Life: What on Earth Am I Here For?* by Rick Warren.

Even though the basis of the book is spiritual, it is probably the most widely purchased book about purpose in history. Warren's message is designed to help people discover their purpose in life so they can be motivated to do something. His book presents purpose as a foundational motivating principle. It has sold over twenty million copies, and its success is empirical proof of the desire people have to put some kind of meaningful structure in their lives and to provide them with the ability to make changes in their lives. Warren's book has been purchased by individuals, businesses, and places of worship in large quantities, and it has spawned educational seminars designed to help people as well as organizations apply principles of purpose to their leadership strategies.

When it comes to leadership, the ability to communicate purpose in conjunction with a vision has a powerful effect on others. The reason it is powerful is that purpose provides *specific direction* and it begins to bring *practical application* to a vision. A vision without a specific purpose may come across as a whim, and it's difficult to get people to support a vision like that because it may be difficult to believe. To really achieve clarity, vision and purpose must be linked and articulated. When it happens, voluntary change can happen very quickly.

To understand how purpose can and will contribute to the clarity you have about your vision, you must be able to answer one simple question:

> "Why is what I want important
> to me and to others?"

In simple terms, you have to be able to list specific reasons for doing whatever it is your vision calls you to do:

- Is your vision to become a great business leader?

- If so, what are the reasons you want to become a great business leader?
- What will you get out of being a great leader, and what specific benefits will others get from your being a great leader?
- What specific things do you want to accomplish?
- In the same way, if your vision is to invent something or start a business, what are the reasons you have for doing it?

If you can't articulate specific reasons why your vision is important to you and to others, then you do not understand your purpose. It's also important to understand that purpose is a transcendent concept that actually wraps itself around your vision and carries it. For example, in the case of a war, the *vision* might be to win the war, but the *purpose* of going to war is to preserve freedom. The motivation of preserving freedom (the purpose) actually transcends the vision of winning the war and legitimizes the entire effort. Exercise 8 in Appendix A will help you define your vision's purpose and value, giving it weight and legitimacy.

A Young Man's Vision Becomes Reality: A Case Study

In 2005, Ben Kaufman started a new business while still a freshman in college. He had an idea and convinced his parents to take out a home-equity loan and they gave/loaned him $180,000 to pursue it. In 2006, Kaufman's company earned revenues of approximately $1 million. His company, which he named Mophie, specialized in the creation of iPod accessories. His first product was something called a Song Sling, which allowed iPod users to comfortably and safely carry the device around their necks.

Was Kaufman's vision and purpose to make iPod accessories? No! Kaufman's vision was to revolutionize the way consumer products were developed. His purpose (which transcended his vision) was to create a process to empower consumers to have a larger stake in creating the products they wanted. His iPod products were just a means to an end. His attitude was that the products weren't that important—what mattered was the process.

"*Purpose is a transcendent concept that actually wraps itself around your vision and carries it.*"

After significant success in the first year of his new business, Kaufman rented a booth at the 2007 Macworld Expo and demonstrated the power of his vision. When people came to his booth, he merely handed them paper and a pencil and asked them to sketch their idea for an iPod accessory they would like to have. In four hours, he collected 120 new product ideas for iPod accessories.

That night, Kaufman put the images up on his company Web site and asked the expo attendees to vote for the best doodles. The result of the process was a line of three new products. In just three days, Kaufman moved new products from design to the marketplace. His purpose of empowering consumers to better impact the products they wanted was a reality.

As Kaufman's process matured, he sold his iPod product line and started a new online business called Kluster. At the 2008 Technology, Entertainment, and Design Conference, Kaufman linked 2,700 people from 104 countries together in a computer forum to brainstorm a new product. They were given parameters about product objectives, product size, and materials that could be used. Kaufman's group settled on producing a board game that was linked to the conference theme.

Within seventy-two hours, Kaufman took the conference stage with a fully modeled prototype of the game and told the audience, "This is what you guys made." Today, Kaufman is using Kluster to help companies link up in real time with their real customers to quickly develop and produce products that are certain to sell: "His purpose of empowering consumers to better impact the products they wanted was a reality."

The purpose that transcended his vision enabled Kaufman to transition his business from making iPod accessories to something more significant. Kaufman said recently, "Our products aren't important, it's our process, which is to listen and respond." Kaufman is twenty-one years old and ranked No. 1 on *Inc.* magazine's list of Top 30 Entrepreneurs Under 30.

Though vision is important, *purpose* can transcend it. A strong purpose will empower you to reach success not previously expected or even thought possible. Once you really understand why you are pursuing your vision, new and greater opportunities will present themselves, and you'll be ready to capitalize on them.

Value: Articulating Felt Needs

What + Why	
Purpose + **Value**	= Clarity

When you think about value, what is your understanding of that word? When you compare it to price, or to desire, does that influence your understanding? A great need of business today is to train business development teams to market and sell *value* over *price*. Competition is squeezing margins tighter than at any previous time in history, and businesses have discovered that strategically selling value is their best reasonable hope to increase margins and profits.

Value is an issue of perception. When sales are made based on higher perceived value, people will pay more for a product. It is unfortunate that many businesses have difficulty articulating their value proposition in a powerful way. This is particularly true of businesses that offer services. Many lack clarity as to what their value proposition really is, or should be, and they have great difficulty putting it into words. They continually search for the elusive thirty-second elevator speech that makes a powerful statement about what they do and the value they bring to the marketplace. They intuitively have an idea about what it might be, but they have a hard time putting it into words.

The difficulty in producing this kind of effective language is caused by not being able to grasp the issues the value proposition must address. Organizations need a value proposition containing language that impacts the listener at the level of "felt need" (which was discussed in Chapter 2). Far too many leaders and business development professionals don't have clarity about what *felt need* is. Therefore, they don't understand how to clearly communicate and impact the most perceived needs of the people to whom they are trying to sell. This challenge is most significant for companies that offer intangible products or services.

What exactly is a felt need and why is it important? Felt needs are about solutions to problems and challenges. People are instinctively problem/solution–oriented with respect to their thinking. Your problems may be minor or they may be devastatingly serious. Whatever they may be, you intuitively look for solutions for all of them. Long before solutions for significant problems and challenges are discovered, you usually feel like you need something new to provide solutions you can actually implement. In these situations, you are usually pretty clear about the need for a new solution because the results you are experiencing are not acceptable. Past solutions are no longer working. You are feeling and experiencing the symptoms and the results of some unresolved problem or challenge.

When you experience problems, a typical response is to try to come up with solutions that will fix the problem. This happens in a variety of ways. You have discussions with other people. You might conduct some research. More likely, you will just use your own experience, reasoning ability, and common sense to figure out what needs to be done to fix the problem. Usually you can figure out something that will work reasonably well and can overcome the problem.

However, there are times when nothing seems to work, and the problem just goes on and on and on. When that condition persists, the elusive solution to your challenge becomes one of your basic felt needs. You can describe the symptoms and everything you may have tried to fix the problem, but you can't articulate an exact prescription to fix it. This is the point when the student is ready, and it is time for a teacher to appear.

Consultants are often hired because people have exhausted their own solutions. Consultants are often able to demonstrate their understanding of the primary felt needs of their customer and to offer solutions their customer believes will work. When customers hear their felt need clearly stated and also hear a solution they intuitively believe will work, the result is an "aha!" experience, which is the connection of problem and solution. It is epiphany. It is perceived value.

The Relationship of Value to Results

When I was a kid, my dad taught the most important business principle of my life: *"Give value: Do more than is expected!"* For individuals and businesses to realize their vision and truly succeed, this principle should drive all thought processes. It is the foundation of whatever success I have enjoyed, and in fact, my entire business centers on helping my clients develop and execute their visions based on that idea.

Leadership is a results contest. If leaders don't deliver results, they are asked to step down and are replaced by others. In the case of the self-employed, if they don't deliver results, they go out of business. A powerful concept every leader must understand is the relationship of value to results. As investor, businessman, and philanthropist Warren Buffett stated so well:

> "Price is what you pay;
> value is what you get."

We've all heard the term *"buyer's remorse."* I think it is a polite term for the way people feel when they have purchased something and the item or the experience did not meet their felt needs and expectations. In many instances, this disappointment accelerates through remorse and becomes anger. We have all found ourselves in this disappointing condition, and it's all about value. Did we get what we wanted, and did the product or service meet or exceed our felt needs and expectations? The negatives of disappointment are significant, but there is a huge positive impact on results when products or services exceed value expectations.

Think about this: When a product or service meets customers' expectations, those customers will be satisfied with their purchase, and they will not feel remorse about the purchase. However, if the product or service merely meets an expectation, it will not always translate into growth for the business. Just meeting an expectation doesn't get people excited. They are merely *satisfied* with what they got for their money. They won't necessarily become a raving fan and tell others about the product or service. Worse, they remain open to the sales and marketing efforts of competitors and are more likely to buy based on price, rather than on value. People who are merely satisfied are people who can be influenced by your competitors who are able to sell on the basis of value. These are the people who can shift market-share percentages when they move their allegiance to products or services that promise to *exceed their expectations* through *greater value*.

> **❝We should all strive to exceed expectations, *and this really is possible only when operating with absolute clarity.*❞**

When we buy something that exceeds our expectations, we are *blown away* by our good fortune. We can't believe that we "got all of this" for what we paid. What we got could be a combination of product quality, customer support, the effect the product had on our lives, or any other thing that makes us happy about the money we spent. When our expectations are exceeded, we become walking advertisements and testimonials for the product or service. Every time we run across a friend with a similar need, we tell them about what we got for what we paid. We are raving fans at that point, and a raving fan can't be tempted and lured away by competitors. This is the kind of customer that leads to growth and great results for any business.

We should all strive to *exceed expectations*, and this really is possible only when operating with absolute clarity. It's simultaneously a goal to pursue and a signal that you're doing things right.

Value in Action: Going for the Green: A Case Study

Smart industries and companies identify the felt needs of their target audiences, based not on guesswork or shareholder goals but instead on information acquired from focus groups and consumer feedback. Among the most innovative and flexible is the American automotive industry, which continually redesigns its offerings. Henry Ford's very first car, the famous Model T, was introduced at a favorably low price point, which appealed to the time's tight economics, and was easy to learn to drive—an important factor, since the entire concept of car ownership was new to the masses. As the success of the Model T soared (sales passed 250,000 in 1914), innovations were made, such as lowering the price and offering other colors beyond the basic black, and the final production of the car was 15,007,034 in 1927.

Since then, automakers have known to listen to the felt needs of drivers. From the early innovations of adding windshields and glove compartments to later adjustments made to please female consumers (for example, Chrysler's La Femme, marketed in the mid-1950s, was a rose-colored vehicle that included a "stunning shoulder bag in soft rose leather . . . fitted with compact, lighter, lipstick and cigarette case"), today's engineers focus largely on energy efficiency and the ability to operate a vehicle using alternative fuels, attempting to create the ideal "green car."

The United States alone consumes 25 percent of the world's oil yet holds only 3 percent of the world's known oil reserves. Therefore, the costs of relying on foreign sources of fuel grow greater each day. Beyond the basic and obvious need to create a car not dependent on petroleum-based fuel are the felt needs of consumers who want to impact the environment less, follow the popular (and peer-pressuring) green movement, and reduce their overall fuel expenses. Meeting those felt needs will provide tremendous value to today's driver.

Although an automobile powered by anything other than gasoline seems like a new idea, it's not. Steam was originally the fuel of choice for "motor carriages," until electric cars took over in the mid-1800s. Even Ford made an electric coupe, but when Ford made cars more accessible and affordable, the electric-car alternative was quickly phased out. In the 1930s, Citroen pioneered diesel-powered passenger cars, an idea other manufacturers tried with middling success until present times.

The 1973 oil crisis led to renewed interest in alternative fuels. To meet consumers' felt needs, manufacturers again tried electric cars, but not until the 1980s and 1990s did the "green car" concept really begin to flourish. Subsequent development included cars powered by solar cells, batteries, and electricity, and now alternative-fuel cars are widely available and wholly a part of the driving mainstream.

Today's consumers can—and do—choose from a variety of reasonably priced hybrids (cars that use minimal gasoline strengthened by a rechargeable energy storage system). As of May 2008, "Reported U.S. sales of hybrids in April climbed 46% to 39,898 units from April 2007. Sales of Toyota's Prius were up 67% to 21,757 units. Toyota has now sold more than 680,000 Priuses in total in the US (more than 514,000 beginning in 2004), and will likely break the 700,000-unit mark next month."[1]

---

1. www.greencarcongress.com/2008/05/reported-us-sal.html#more

True success depends on being nimble in the face of change and sometimes even *seeking* ways to change so you're continually ahead of the curve. Soliciting and listening to the felt needs of the people important to your success, personal or professional, is a great way to determine what and when to change.

Clarity: Pulling You Forward

What + Why	= Clarity
Purpose + Value	

Now that we understand the variables of the Clarity Equation, it's time to turn to clarity itself. The contrast between having clarity and not having clarity is striking, and the effect on reaching your vision (personal or professional) will be dramatic. Sometimes we think we have clarity when we really haven't initially considered it at all. We haven't asked ourselves, *"What do I really want and why do I want it?"* Not being clear at the outset will create significant repercussions as you go about attempting to reach your goals and realize your vision.

Many people start down their goal path without having clarity, either believing they have clarity when they don't or not even thinking about it at all. Over the past two decades, many of my clients have felt that they clearly understood what they wanted and where they needed to go, when in actuality their understanding of their vision was muddled. They lacked *real* clarity and asked me to help define what they wanted to pursue and why they wanted to pursue it.

For a business, the absence of clarity can have subtle but serious repercussions. Organizational energy and forward propulsion will be halted. Leaders and teams will procrastinate, sit idle, and feel frustrated. Personally, not having clarity will have similar effects that slow progress and push the vision farther and farther from being realized.

When I work with people who lack clarity, I facilitate some eye-opening exercises (which are discussed in detail in Appendix A) that remove impurities from the overall vision and help solidify the "why." This begins to develop clarity, and soon amazing and wholesale changes begin to occur. In my client experiences, procrastination evaporated. Organizational energy was amplified and rejuvenated. Action became the watchword, the driving focus. And best of all, my clients began to consistently exceed expectations, their own and those of others. That alone may be the most important hallmark of working with true clarity.

Tactical vs. Strategic Thinking

The amount of money spent on improvement and training each year is immense. The purpose of the investment is to acquire specific skills that will improve results and outcomes. Most improvement offerings are about how to do specific things better in order to be more effective. In sales training, this might involve learning how to write a more powerful cold-call letter or overcome objections. For a manager, tactical skills might involve learning how to better lead meetings or serve as a mentor. Personally, we might take classes to cook healthier meals or better manage household finances. These are all ways to become more *tactically* effective.

Throughout my career, however, I have learned that a better improvement objective is for people to become more *strategically* effective. This means acquiring new ways of thinking, not just new ways of doing things. And specifically, for the purposes of Strategic Acceleration, I'm talking about new ways to think about clarity.

A shift from focusing on the tactical to focusing on the strategic is a change of mind-set that has far-reaching effects and benefits, instead of a "one-off" approach that has short-term reach. For example, instead of writing a better pitch letter, a sales rep would learn how to put his mind into that of his customer and to truly relate and build rapport. A manager would become a self-assured leader and mentor. A parent would provide a lifestyle of smart money management and healthy choices. It's about wholesale changes in philosophy and priorities. It's about clarity of the what and the why.

Consequences of Not Having Clarity

My nature is to be a positive encourager, so I don't want to dwell too much on the negative. However, we all have experienced setbacks at some time in our lives, and it is a reality that must be considered. There are lots of reasons traditionally given for not reaching our goals, but many of them are just symptoms of a deeper root cause: a lack of clarity. Here are three symptoms of poor clarity:

1. **People don't believe they can do what they have to do:** For example, when sports teams enter a championship game, a team that does not believe it can win will not win. In the same way, people must believe they can execute a vision, or they will not be able to do it. When you don't believe you can do what you have to do, it means you don't believe in yourself or your vision. This means that *you don't have clarity about what you really want.*
2. **People use planning to avoid taking action:** Preparation and planning are important, but excessive preparation is nothing more than procrastination. It is only when you start doing what you need to do that you can begin to produce results. If you procrastinate, it often

means you are fearful of failure and may not be confident of your ability to succeed. Clarity destroys procrastination because the action you need to take is vividly clear. It pulls you forward and eliminates the need to be pushed. *Procrastination is a primary symptom of the need to push or be pushed.*

3. **People quit or give up in the face of adversity or difficulty:** It is always easy to quit, and too many people prefer quitting to the discomfort they experience when the going gets tough. The reason is simple: Adversity is painful. For example, businesses that lack the perseverance to be competitive in a rapidly changing economy will have serious problems. When you quit in the face of adversity, it means *you are deficient in the mental substance it takes to persevere and overcome. Clarity* is the missing ingredient.

All three of these reasons for failure are the result of a mental approach that suffers from a lack of clarity. Therefore, the single most significant thing you can do to ensure against failure is to achieve clarity.

> **"**A goal properly set
> is halfway reached.**"**
> —Zig Ziglar

If-Then Thinking

When a plan or strategy goes sour and the results are less than expected, the planners soon find themselves trying to explain how it happened. What usually follows are lengthy bouts of what I call "if-then" thinking. *"If I had known this, then I could've/should've/would've done that."* "If-then" thinking is the direct result of poor clarity. Having clarity during any planning process will significantly reduce the incidence of "if-then" thinking because the plan is more likely to be executed successfully. So, if clarity is the solution, you have to ask if there is a factual way to know you have it. Fortunately, the answer is yes, it is a verifiable condition.

Many people believe they have clarity when they have produced goals and have worked out the necessary action steps. These tools are important, but they are more directly related to your ability to *focus* and keep that focus on the main things. You must know two points to produce clarity:

1. Where you want to be when your vision becomes reality
2. An objective understanding of current conditions

These two points must be described in words that can be easily understood, and they must be wrapped with understanding the "why." You must understand *why* you want to go where you want to go, and you must understand *why* you are where you are today. Exercise 7 in Appendix A will walk you through an analysis of current strengths, weaknesses, opportunities, and threats. This will help you clarify the "why" of things and more fully expand your understanding of your vision's purpose and value. From there, in Exercise 8, you'll document that purpose and value, and begin to build your personal Clarity Equation.

The Practical Effect of Clarity

One of the great joys of my own work is seeing the transforming power of clarity in my clients' lives and businesses—and how fast it happens. One of my recent clients was the

Canadian company Libertas Holdings, a diversified real estate investment firm that handles investments, asset acquisition, brokerage, and property management. The two principals of Libertas are Tyler Uzelman and Keenan Tameling. I asked Tyler and Keenan to share their experience about the effect clarity had on their business. They provided the following to help you see the practical effect of clarity and what it has empowered them to do and be.

> We were originally referred to Tony by a business friend and associate who had known him for a number of years. He told us that Tony could help us take our business to a new level. At the time, we actually thought we were pretty clear in our direction and were a bit skeptical about how much an outside party could help us. However, we had confidence in our friend and engaged Tony's assistance. We flew from our offices in Canada to Tony's Strategic Acceleration Studio in Dallas. Although we were only there one day, the experience literally transformed our business, and it happened as a result of elevating our clarity and focus!
>
> Becoming more clear about our purpose (why our vision is important), our value (why our vision's success is important to and will benefit others), and the details of what we need to be doing (actions and tasks necessary to reaching our success) has rapidly changed the way we do everything. Before working with Tony, we had a view that was farther into the future than we could really see. We were focusing on the long-term financial growth of the enterprise on the basis of net worth and asset acquisition. The clarity we got, however, was on the need to build up the cash-generation capabilities of the business through the property management division. Essentially,

we changed our short-term focus to greatly change our long-term outcome, much to our financial delight!

We compare the clarity process Tony gave us with going to an optometrist to get a new pair of glasses. When you first look through the eye exam machine at the letter chart on the wall, the images are very fuzzy. Then, the optometrist begins flipping through different lenses for each eye. Every lens flip brings the chart into sharper focus. Eventually, the image is so clear, you can read the fine print at the bottom of the chart. That is what the clarity process was like for us. We thought we could see pretty clearly, but we were really just looking at the biggest letters at the top of the chart. Now we can really see the fine print.

One of the most amazing effects of clarity has been the removal of stress from us personally, and for our team. We now understand the why and how of all we do, and there is little that is unknown. This level of clarity has eliminated feelings of uncertainty about the future and imparts huge levels of confidence about what we are doing. Tony's concept that clarity pulls you toward your vision and that you no longer feel pushed is completely accurate, and that is exactly what we have experienced. When you have clarity as we learned through Strategic Acceleration, things become much simpler. You don't have to be the smartest, hardest-working person in the world to be wildly successful. The path is just there before you, and you follow it. All you have to do is take the steps that clarity has illuminated for you.

The effect of clarity on our team has been amazing. We are not the same company we were. Our meetings have become entirely different. We used to come together to talk about where everybody was and what they were up to. Now we come together in a proactive way and talk about opportunities. It's like we are now ahead of the power curve and not behind it. We are being pulled forward, rather than pushed. We are proactive, not reactive. Everybody knows what they have to do. We spend our time talking about where we are going, rather than where we have been.

Another thing that is different is that we now ask ourselves "why" about everything that comes up. If it does not have purpose, value, and relevance, it's not a priority. Clarity has also had a powerful impact on our vision for the business. We no longer see ourselves as a company serving a specific geographic niche in Canada. We ultimately see ourselves as a national enterprise. We can do what we do everywhere. Our revenues will easily double over the next 18 months and maybe more. Doubling is a conservative estimate. If it quadruples, we will not be surprised, based on what is happening right now. We know this is the result of the new clarity and focus that we have about everything.

The purpose and value of all that we do is known to our entire company, and that has produced the high level of clarity we now have. We are a more confident organization. We are really good at what we do and frankly, don't believe we have much competition.

Isn't that a powerful illustration about the practical effect clarity can have on an organization? You can see by Keenan and Tyler's remarks that understanding purpose and value are the key ingredients that enabled them to "flip the clarity lenses" and develop the ability to read the fine print of their future. They were able to share this transformation within weeks of their clarity enhancement experience in Dallas.

For you, this means that you need to define your vision and why you want it, as well as its purpose and value. This can be accomplished by considering the following questions:

1. What do you really want, personally or professionally? ("What")
2. Why do you want it? ("Why")
3. Why is your vision important to you? ("Purpose")
4. Why is your success important to others? ("Value")

Defining the above will enable you to build a Clarity Equation of your own, which is another crucial step toward realizing your vision.

Clarity and Performance

Clarity actually provides a specific kind of power whose absence is painful, for it's manifested in human performance. In any endeavor, certain intangible human qualities must drive the effort. People have to *believe in* what they are doing. They must be *committed to achievement*. There must be a certain amount of *mental toughness and resilience* to persevere through difficulties and roadblocks. A certain amount of legitimate *excitement* never hurts either. True clarity as I define it contributes to creating all these qualities, and with these qualities comes power—the power to produce results.

The power produced when clarity is achieved creates real effects within a business or organization. The effects are always positive. The first effect is a boost in organizational energy. People know what to do, and they are motivated to action. When people understand the "why" of things (purpose and value), the combination produces a level of clarity that has enough influence to actually become motivational! It becomes the fuel of voluntary change and enables you to be *pulled* toward your vision, rather than pushed. It produces behavior that is the exact opposite of passive rebellion, and it becomes a positive affirmation that leads to *proactive attitudes* and *voluntary change*.

Summary

Clarity has the power to pull you forward to your vision, rather than having to be pushed. To have clarity about your vision, you must understand where you want to be and where you are today. You also need to understand why you should proceed to pursue the vision, and that is found in purpose and value. The purpose of your vision is discovered when you know why it is important to yourself and others, and value is found in the felt needs you want to meet. These are the elements of clarity. Do you have it?

The next section of the book discusses focus, the second component of Strategic Acceleration. You will develop the ability in the next chapter to identify and concentrate on what really matters for the success of your vision—perhaps the greatest catalyst for change and success I can teach you.

Very Important Points

▶ Many people believe they have clarity when they have produced goals and have worked out the necessary action steps. These tools are important, but they are more directly related to your ability to focus and keep that focus on the main things. You must know two points to produce clarity:

1. Where you want to be when your vision becomes reality
2. An objective understanding of current conditions

▶ A vision without a specific purpose may come across as a whim, and it's difficult to get people to support a vision like that because it may be difficult to believe. To really achieve clarity, vision and purpose must be linked and articulated. When it happens, voluntary change can happen very quickly.

▶ The basic definition of clarity is: having *an unfettered view of your vision*, which is what you want and why you want it, fed by an understanding of its purpose and value. When people understand the "why" of things (purpose and value), the combination produces a level of clarity that has enough influence to actually become motivational! It becomes the fuel of voluntary change and enables you to be pulled toward your vision, rather than pushed.

CHAPTER 4

Focus Is the Opposite of Distraction

☞ *Success pivots on having the ability to concentrate on doing the things that really matter and filtering out what doesn't.*

Chapters 1–3 described the importance of developing *clarity* about your vision, as well as understanding the "why" behind it. A clear and authentic vision enables willing changes in behavior and sets you up for success. Gaining clarity on your vision, however, is just the first step in the Strategic Acceleration process. The second step, *focus*, is the topic of Chapters 4 and 5, which will teach you how to better develop this important skill. Once you have the ability to focus on your vision (and all of the strategies, tactics, and actions required for its success), you will be ready for the final step, *execution*, or acting on and accomplishing your vision.

This chapter shows you how to identify and concentrate on what really matters for the success of your vision, and filter out the distractions that hinder its progress. Success truly hinges on the ability to cut through the clutter, drown out the noise, and focus on the high-leverage activities that are the backbone of reaching your vision.

❝*Learn to say 'no' to the good*
*so you can say 'yes' to the best.***❞**
—John C. Maxwell

Have you ever attended an NBA basketball game? In the final minutes of close games, the team that is behind usually resorts to a strategy of committing intentional fouls on the other team. When a player is fouled, the game clock is stopped to allow the fouled player to attempt one or more free throws. What the free-throw shooter sees is the basket against a backdrop of several thousand frenzied lunatic fans waving towels, tassels, pom-poms, or anything else they have been able to bring into the arena to distract the shooter from making the free throw. The fans scream, yell, blast air horns, and do anything they can to break the shooter's concentration. To be successful, the shooter has to block all of this mayhem from his mind and focus on the basket.

The most focused players in the NBA are able to make 90 percent of their free throws. The least focused players make less than 50 percent of their attempts. The point of this illustration is that you have to keep your eye on the goal to be successful, and that requires a way to maintain your focus in the midst of distractions.

Learning How to Focus

Focus is not something that comes naturally for most people, and that is why it is a skill that must be learned, polished, and practiced. Specifically, focus is a thinking skill that is acquired as a result of mental discipline. To develop mental discipline concerning focus, you have to treat it the same way you would acquire any skill. If you recall the discussion of the Effectiveness Ladder presented in Chapter 1, you will better understand the process you need to follow to acquire focusing skills:

- Become aware of the need to improve your focusing skills
- Clarify the need, and make a conscious decision to invest the time and energy needed to improve your skills
- Focus on the need, and practice and train your mind to focus
- Execute the solution by implementing your new skills and making them a routine that is second nature

This chapter uses the Effectiveness Ladder as a template to explain how you can improve this vital, strategic skill and help others do the same.

Rung #1: Become Aware of the Need for Focus

Jon, an educated and intelligent mechanical engineer who attends my church, is a rising star in the oil and gas industry. He is considered an expert in designing heat exchangers, which are extremely expensive, custom-built pieces of process equipment that allow for the efficient transfer of heat and energy between two separate fluids. The design of these contraptions is a complex process that involves, among many other tasks, determining needs gathered from several sources; examining and analyzing the properties of the fluids involved; deciding which design would be most appropriate for the site and budget; working with vendors and suppliers to gather machinery and materials; and refining the design to ensure its efficiency, proper operation, and timely delivery.

In effect, he sifts through probably four hundred pieces of information from internal and external sources to build a machine that, if badly designed or improperly constructed, could cause tremendous negative financial impact. This is a process that requires sharp focus and attention to detail. And although he's been trained to perform this process, and he consistently produces good designs, he told me that he initially found the process overwhelming due to an inability to fully focus.

> **"***Focus is not something that comes naturally for most people, and that is why it is a skill that must be learned, polished, and practiced.***"**

While he was thinking through every minute detail in designing this machinery, Jon was constantly barraged by colleagues, his land line, his cell phone, instant messaging chimes, e-mail notifications, package deliveries, text messages, others' conversations in the hallway or adjacent offices, and every other distraction common in all of our workdays. When he finally found a quiet moment to think through complex design specifications or review lengthy bids from vendors, his manager would want to discuss his personal life, his wife would instant message him about dinner decisions, and he'd get seven "urgent" e-mails.

Although he fully recognized his vision and priorities (to design a heat exchanger quickly and properly), he was unable to efficiently do so because of interruptions and distractions that were not at all critical to his vision. Without focus, he simply could not perform his job well, which would impact his career path, financial gain, and overall satisfaction. He needed focus, and he knew it.

Determining the need for focus initially involves understanding that focus is a strategic skill. It also involves understanding how well—or how poorly—you currently focus. That means conducting an inventory of what you currently believe (your belief window, described in detail in Chapter 2) about your ability to focus. To help him better understand the strategic nature of focus, I urged Jon to ask himself the following questions:

- How well do you focus throughout the day?
- How well does your organization focus on the priorities that produce success?
- Are you really aware of how many minutes a day you lose because of distractions?
- Do you really understand the huge benefits you will enjoy when you can eliminate distractions that have a negative impact on the results you achieve?

You, too, should consider these questions. Getting to the bottom of these issues is the first step you must take to discover the strategic nature of focus.

Most people don't think of focus as a strategic skill, and most people haven't really spent much time factually examining how well they focus. Focus is a subject that gets a lot of lip service, but it usually doesn't get the respect it deserves. When you don't treat focus as a strategic issue, minimizing its importance is easy, and soon you're ignoring it altogether. Most people approach focus as a time-management issue or as an organizational challenge. Typical solutions to improve focus may include obtaining a better time-management system, or doing something to better organize the work environment. These are valid considerations, but those kinds of solutions don't address the heart of the focus issue, which is distraction!

Distraction is a natural occurrence in every person's life. You can be the most organized person on Earth, with a great time-management system, and still become routinely distracted.

Since distraction is the opposite of focus, your ability to focus is directly related to how well you are able to consistently avoid and eliminate distractions. The problem is that your mind functions in a way that naturally invites distraction, and it is caused by the very strengths that make your brain so amazing. Because your brain functions as a connector of concepts, facts, and events, it is the master collection bucket of your five senses and absorbs everything you experience for processing. In one sense, the brain is constantly seeking input to process, and it has a voracious appetite for that input.

> **"**Since distraction is the opposite
> of focus, your ability to focus is
> directly related to how well you
> are able to consistently avoid
> and eliminate distractions.**"**

Information and input is the raw material for human creativity, opportunity recognition, and problem solving. That's the good news. Unfortunately, distraction is the direct result of the same brain function. That's the bad news. You become distracted whenever you allow something to enter your mind that takes you away from doing what you should be doing in the present moment. In fact, distraction is the path of least resistance because the most natural activity for your mind is to take in information. Unfortunately, that is all you need to latch onto things that can remove you from the moment and disrupt whatever focus you had for the immediate task at hand. In other words, distraction is a natural result of thinking! Your ability to overcome distraction and elevate your focusing skill depends on your ability to learn how to think in ways that will counteract what comes so naturally.

One of the challenges of living in the information age is the extraordinary number of opportunities you have to become distracted. The very things that are meant to be powerful tools to help you be more effective are potential sources of distraction. The Internet, e-mail, and cell phones all introduce unexpected intrusions into our minds, and every intrusion creates the possibility of disrupting your ability to focus on what you really should be doing at the moment. Focus is about establishing priorities and keeping the main things in front of you. To do that effectively, you have to be able to control the distractive influences that bombard your mind. Your ability to do that depends on how you think about the present moment, because focus is always found in the present.

How well do you focus? Only one objective standard can measure your ability to focus, and that standard involves *the ability to consistently complete predetermined objectives on time.* People who are consistently late for meetings, late for telephone appointments, and late finishing projects and tasks have a focus deficiency. Focus is also a problem for those who are consistently behind in their work and constantly scrambling to meet deadlines. I'm not saying that you will never experience times when you have more on your plate than you can handle. I'm talking about when those conditions are a way of life! Some people are always harried and behind the power curve of getting things done. That condition is a hallmark of a focus deficiency.

To help you determine how well you focus, I challenge you to keep a Focus Journal for two weeks. It is easy to do, but you will have to focus on your real activities and exercise discipline to get it done. All you need to do is keep a daily log of your activities. Just write down your priorities for each day and the specific things you intend to *finish* each day. Then keep an activity log of all that happens to you during the day. Be particularly mindful to log each distraction you experience and the amount of time you invested in the distraction. If you keep this log faithfully for two weeks, you will have a clear picture of what is going on in your life each day concerning focus. When you can see that, you will understand your need to improve. Exercise 10 in Appendix B provides a Focus Journal template and example that will help you take this important step.

Rung #2: Clarify the Need to Improve Your Focus Skills

Jon, our engineer from earlier, knew he needed to focus better. Continual interruptions were seriously affecting his ability to perform his job well, but he also realized that a distraction-free work environment was impossible and unrealistic. He thought about the kinds of distractions that affected his ability to focus on his design process, and on my advice, he kept a two-week Focus Journal. He quickly saw that every day, seemingly insignificant distractions really added up. He spent probably three to four cumulative hours a day being pulled in every conceivable direction *except* toward realizing his goal. As he reviewed his journal, he considered that some of these interruptions could probably be mitigated, others eliminated. But which ones? He knew he needed to change how he conducted his workday. But how to do it? "Change is hard!" he said. He wondered whether the effort would pay off.

As you approach the second rung on the Effectiveness Ladder, you now understand your need for focus. You understand that focus is jeopardized by distraction and that focus is an acquired skill. The next step is to clarify your need so you can make good choices about what you need to *do* about it. Remember, this is the rung on the ladder where you make a commitment to improve your ability to focus. It will not be simple or completely painless, and it will require a willingness to change the way you do some very basic things. Remember the discussion we had in Chapters 1 and 2 about voluntary change and the importance of willingness? A commitment to improve your ability to focus engages those principles.

When you complete the two-week Focus Journal mentioned earlier in this chapter, you should have a clear picture of how well you currently focus. You will also be positioned to make an informed choice about your commitment to improvement.

To help you make the choice to improve your focus, simply return mentally to all the work you have done to achieve clarity about what you really want. Having that clarity will help you keep in view the priorities that will carry you to your strategic objectives. In contrast, without focus, your results will be limited, and the time it takes to achieve the results you seek will be significantly extended. What is the benefit of getting clear on what you want if you are unwilling to do the work it takes to attain it? Remember, Strategic Acceleration is about getting superior results faster. The ability to focus is one of the critical success factors that help you do that, because focus has the effect of increasing time. It's not that you will actually have more time in your day. Each day has twenty-four hours, and that will not change. However, focus gives you the power to make better use of those hours, and if you can consistently increase what you accomplish as a result of improving your focus, the effect is like adding time to your day.

Therefore, getting clear on your need to improve your ability to focus involves accepting that you might be allowing distractions to steal many minutes from every day. Exercise 11 in Appendix B will help you with the following review of your Focus Journal and help you improve your focus skills.

When you complete your Focus Journal, look at how many minutes each day you lost to distractions that barged into your mind and led you on unplanned activities. Specifically, take a closer look at the priorities you established for each day and the specific things you intended to *finish* each day. Make a list of the priorities and tasks that you did not complete on the day in question, and then subject each of them to a couple of tough questions—ask yourself:

- Why didn't I complete the work I had prioritized to complete each day?
- What happened that caused me not to complete them?
- Write down specific answers to these questions and evaluate those answers as distractions. Regardless of how legitimate they look, if they caused you to not finish what you planned to finish, they were a distraction and caused you to lose your focus.

You should now have enough information to be clear about your need to improve your ability to focus. Your Focus Journal will have exposed your focus challenge, and you should be able to make a good decision about making the commitment to improve your focus skills:

- Do you need to improve your focus skills?
- Do you see the value in improving those skills?
- Are you willing to do it?

If you answered *yes*, you are ready for Rung #3 on the Effectiveness Ladder.

Rung #3: Focus on Improving Your Skills, Then Practice

Jon had committed to making some changes in his daily routine that better suited his vision. He was ready to fully concentrate and to eliminate or put aside many of the distractions that affected his work. He decided to devote six hours a day to his design responsibilities, with a one-hour personal break dividing the six hours, and one hour at the end of the day to catch up on noncritical, work-related activities. During those "design hours," as he called them, he closed his office door, quit his e-mail and instant messaging applications, and turned off the ringer on his phone. He also communicated to his colleagues that a closed door meant "Please do not disturb unless truly an emergency." He forced himself, every day, to begin with a prioritized to-do list, keep to his schedule, and not deviate from his plan to take control of his distractions.

To improve your focusing skills, you need practice, practice, practice! The nature of the practice regarding focus is mental because *distraction* is mental. You must learn how to mentally screen distractions as they arise and develop the ability to push through those distractions so you can keep the focus on the main thing.

Your Focus Journal will be a beginning, but it will deal with simple daily to-do's, not the strategic, high-leverage activities that deserve the lion's share of your time and attention. Don't misunderstand: Daily to-do's are important, and they are the small building blocks for the eventual success of your vision, but the real strategic measure of your focus will be found at a higher level. Chapter 5 will teach you how to identify the specific high-leverage activities that require your focus, but for now, all you need to do is understand their significance.

Activity is not an equal-opportunity function, because some activities have a higher impact on results than others.

For example, in a sales situation, contacting and setting appointments with new customers is a higher-leverage activity than polishing up a PowerPoint presentation. Both activities are important, but increased revenue is a direct result of adding new customers, so it makes sense to spend more time on that activity. The higher-leverage activity should be a higher priority.

Therefore, a big part of your practice to improve your focus skills involves identifying the high-leverage activities that can significantly impact results and making them your daily action priorities. Using the sales example, a significant amount of time each day should be reserved for contacting new customers, and during the time reserved for that activity, your focus needs to be fixed on that alone.

Whether you're in sales or are an executive or an entrepreneur, you have high-leverage activities to identify and focus on. I suggest you make those activities a significant part of every day, and your practice to improve focus should use those activities as the measuring stick of improvement.

Another thing to practice is the way you think about time, specifically the relationships between the past, the present, and the future. The skill to focus is always in the present, but far too many people invest a high percentage of their time thinking about the past and the future, rather than focusing on what they should be doing *today*. Focus and Strategic Acceleration require that you keep your mental attention and your actions in the present. This sounds simple, but it takes time and practice to perfect.

I'm not saying that all things past and future are bad or disruptive. You most certainly learn from your mistakes, which are in the past. The past also contains the sum total of all your experience, both good and bad, which contributes to your wisdom and all that you believe. So don't discount your past. The future is where your vision resides, and when you have clarity about your vision, it provides the power to pull you toward it. Your vision also helps you judge the correctness of your action steps in the present and helps you establish and maintain the correct priorities. So the past and the future are important, but they also provide a breeding ground for distraction.

> **❝The future is where your vision resides, and when you have clarity about your vision, it provides the power to pull you toward it.❞**

Before we discuss the specific kinds of distractions presented by the past and the future, one very important positive about the future must be clearly stated. Having clarity about your vision of the future is vital to maintaining focus in the present. This truth can be illustrated by a little-known fact about the *Apollo 11* mission (the first manned moon flight) that recently was made public. The moon mission was off course during the entire voyage! The mission control crew at NASA had to make lots of course corrections to ensure the landing happened at the right time and place. A NASA scientist involved in the *Apollo* missions said, "The *Apollo 11* moon launch was off course over 90 percent of the time. But a successful landing was still likely because we knew the exact coordinates of our goal. This allowed us to make adjustments as necessary."

The principle for you to see is that because the NASA engineers knew where they were going, being a bit off course during the trip didn't really matter. As long as they knew and remained focused on the ultimate destination, they could adapt and change direction along the way and still achieve their landing coordinates.

When it comes to your own success, being able to know the exact coordinates of your "landing site" gives you what you need to actually arrive. Knowing the exact coordinates of your "landing site" also gives you the measuring stick to focus on the things that matter and to keep the main things matters of priority. Although you can't state your vision in the same language the NASA engineers would use, the exact coordinates of your landing site can be stated with clarity because you have clarity. You know the "why" of your vision and you understand the purpose and value of it. You are clear about what you really want. Because you are clear about your vision, you can use that clarity to identify distractive influences and discipline yourself to cast them aside.

Although the past and future have some positives, they also create most of the problems that threaten your ability to focus on what is important. Certain thoughts related to the past and future are priority killers that produce powerful mental distractions that can stop you dead in your tracks. I'm talking about the fears and concerns we have regarding the future and the excessive baggage we carry from the past into each new day. Successful people can put the past behind them, although they learn from it. Successful people also do not dwell too much on the speculative nature of the future; their primary focus is on doing what they must do today.

To return to the example that introduced this chapter, when a basketball player stands at the free-throw line preparing to take his shot, thoughts about all the free throws he has missed in the past will produce doubt about making the one at hand. The shooter's thoughts will involve the fear of missing, rather than making the shot. If the player starts to worry about missing the shot, his mind will be open to the fear of losing the game. If the game is lost, his team might be eliminated from the tournament or the playoffs. Allowing thoughts about a loss that has not yet happened will disrupt the player's focus and almost guarantee a missed shot.

We may not be professional basketball players, but we all have to take shots every day. Allowing our minds to run around in the past and the future is certain to disrupt the daily focus we need to achieve superior results.

The Problem of Focusing on the Past

Have you ever had a conversation with someone who had a bad experience in the past and it infects everything about the way they live today? They may have suffered a bad marriage or a financial disaster. They may have had a bad experience with a religion or been abused or taken advantage of by others. Every human being will experience trouble in his or her life, but many people are never able to move beyond those experiences. They import the regrets and anger of those past events into every present moment. They subject their wives, husbands, kids, coworkers, and friends to a way of living designed to prevent any possible repeat of past disasters. If someone stole from them, they vow to never trust anybody again. If they were disappointed by a religion, they dismiss spirituality from their lives forever. They become obsessed by past failures to the extent that they are miserable in the present. Their focus is to protect themselves from harm. All of this causes an inability to focus on today and the priorities of things that are really important. They become focused on self-protection and living on defense.

For example, a good friend of mine does a lot of work with people suffering in troubled marriages. He says the daily conflicts people have in their relationships are always fueled by the same cause: The spouses are incapable of living together peacefully because their minds are absorbed by their anger about the past and their apprehension and fear of the future.

They import all of those past and future thoughts into the reality of their daily lives, and they can't see each other as they are today. The truth of their relationship becomes distorted, and the result is a "two-story" house. She has her story, and he has one, too. Reconciliation is possible only when the stories become one and they begin to live in the reality of today and focus on what really matters.

The negative influences of the past foster anger and second-guessing, which themselves often create blame and an inability to see things the way they really are. The lesson is this:

Learn from the past, but leave blame and resentment behind!

The desire to blame creates the if-then thinking we discussed in Chapter 3:

- "*If* only someone had done something different, *then* I would not have had that problem!"
- "*If* my father had been nicer to me, *then* I could be nicer to my own children."
- "*If* my phone would stop ringing, *then* I could concentrate better!"

Whenever you hear if-then words coming from your mouth or the mouths of others, take heed. These words open the front door to all kinds of things that have the power to disrupt your focus and distract you from what has meaning and importance. The solution is to remember that the past is over and can never be changed or relived. It is fruitless to waste time and energy on what might have been.

The Problem of Focusing on the Future

For the most part, the future is a place of uncertainty. It has not yet happened. Attempts to predict the future are based on assumptions about future conditions; if the conditions change, your predictions about the future will be wrong. The future is also capable of creating irrational fear, which always opens the door for mental distractions. These mental distractions are the enemy of focus. We are all familiar with what we call daydreaming. In the midst of doing something, our minds suddenly begin to wander off, and we get lost in a sequence of thoughts that take us nowhere. Usually this condition is provoked by some thought or piece of information that just pops into your mind from nowhere.

For example, let's say you are sitting at home watching TV when a thought suddenly comes into your mind. You think, "Hmmm, I forgot to finish that report that was due yesterday." You then begin to remember other times in the past when you were late doing things and you remember being told by your boss that late submissions might ultimately lead to a career change. You begin to imagine that when you get to work the next day, you are going to be fired. Unemployment will cause you many problems. You just bought a new car, and if you aren't working, you won't be able to make the payments. You consider that the bank is certain to come get the car, and then you will be without transportation. Without a car, you won't even be able to look for a new job. Without a job, you won't be able to pay rent and will probably be evicted. Your spouse and kids will probably leave you, too!

All of this fantasy thinking got started by dwelling on one fact and then projecting assumptions into the future. Emotionally, you actually feel unemployed, on-foot, homeless, and abandoned. None of what you feel or think is based on anything real, but you are left emotionally distracted from the present. This imaginary scenario of you in your living room demonstrates how you can think your way into distractions that destroy your focus.

We all want to be in control of our lives, but achieving that control is impossible if we allow our thinking to bounce back and forth between the past and the future. When we do that, we hop right over *today*, which is the only place we can really do anything that has significance. The only thing in life we can control is what we do from moment to moment, and that is the bottom line of focus:

> Focus is found in the ability to block out all the things we don't like about yesterday and the things we worry about tomorrow and to do the next correct thing we need to do today.

Rung #4: Execute Your Solution and Make It a Second-Nature Routine

Jon continued to work on sticking to his schedule and reducing distractions. Focusing in three-hour chunks of time was mentally manageable for him, especially because he realized he had a "reward" in the form of a break waiting on the other side. Although initially he had trouble being disciplined enough to not check e-mail or occasionally surf the Web for sports scores, he eventually got into the habit of devoting all of his mental energy to his design tasks, eliminating opportunities for noncritical interruptions, and willingly putting distractions aside until another time. He continued to keep his Focus Journal, making daily prioritized to-do lists, and critically examining his journal at the end of each day to determine how to better refine his time.

Within six weeks, he was more focused, productive, and satisfied with his performance. He had successfully designed several heat exchangers before their due dates, and he was able to take on additional design responsibilities because of his now-habitual efficiencies. His manager was extremely pleased with his productivity and urged others in the organization to follow Jon's example.

Rung #4 on the Effectiveness Ladder is not so much an action step as it is a point of arrival. You arrive when you are able to execute your newfound focusing skills with little conscious effort: As mentioned in Chapter 1, it's second nature to you now. It's like taking the training wheels off a bicycle and riding it without effort or conscious thought. When you are able to execute your effectiveness, you will have become a focused person.

Everything you can control about your life happens as a result of your habits, which are the behaviors that define your personality, your relationships, and your effectiveness. The truth is that your success (or failure) is created by your habits, and to get superior results faster, you have to continue to acquire new habits. Improving your focus skills is no different—focus has to become an exceptional new habit for you.

It is very important that you understand that focus is a skill, and skills are the result of habitual action. I say this because acquiring good habits gives your life stability and a sense of peace, for habits make it possible to predict results. Most of us want to be in control of our lives and our future, and we try lots of things to help us achieve that control. We try to get better control through improved filing systems, a more advanced piece of software, a more capable cell phone, and many other things. Most of these aids do help, but we should approach the control issue from the perspective of creating new habits.

In Chapter 1, we discussed the strategic importance of your belief window and how the things you believe drive the action you take and the results you get. Another way of understanding that is to see that your belief window is also the basis for your habits, which largely control what you say and do. If it's true to say, "*If you keep doing the same things over and over again, you will keep getting the same results,*" then results are predictable. This quote is usually made in a negative sense about negative habits, but it is also true about positive habits. If results are predictable, you have the ability to control your future, and more control over your future contributes to peace of mind and happiness.

With respect to focus, four strategic facts and characteristics about your behavior will confirm your ability to execute and focus at a higher level. Let's take a look at those four characteristics, listed below.

Four Positive Characteristics of the Ability to Focus

1. Fewer distractions:

You will have become acutely aware of distractions in real time, as they barge into your mind and your life. As a result, you will be less vulnerable to things that can lure you into time-wasting activities. The key to eliminating distractions is the ability to recognize them. When you have reached this stage of effectiveness, you will intuitively know what distractions look, taste, feel, and smell like! The moment a potential distraction rears its ugly head, you will be able to recoil from it and set it aside in your mind.

2. More high-leverage activities:

You will be intimately aware of the activities for which you need to allocate most of your time and effort. This awareness will help you delegate or ignore tasks and time-eating activities that have minimal impact on achieving superior results. Your priority selection will be greatly enhanced, which means you will be more effective at keeping the focus on the main things.

3. On-time performance:

Success and achievement require the ability to achieve predetermined objectives within established time frames, and this ability will increase tremendously as your focusing skills are elevated. You will rarely fail to complete tasks and projects on time. Instead, you will complete your daily to-do lists, rather than carry them over into subsequent days.

4. Increased productivity:

With fewer distractions, you will be able to get more done because you will have achieved more effective use of your time. You will add lots of extra minutes to every day. I wrote a handbook several years ago called *Finding 100 Extra Minutes a Day,* and I can guarantee that level of increased time is possible for just about anyone. You can expect that level of extra time as a result of improving your focusing skills. You can download a free digital copy of the handbook from the Free Resources section of www.tonyjeary.com. Finding 100 extra minutes each workday amounts to almost 450 hours a year. That's the equivalent of adding almost three weeks of time to each year, which could represent more time to be productive and more time to spend with your family.

Summary

No single skill or habit has a more powerful impact on results than the ability to eliminate distractions and focus on the high-leverage activities that have the greatest potential to advance your strategic goals and objectives. When your ability to do that becomes a habit, your entire life will change, and the results you achieve will be Strategically Accelerated.

Knowing what to reduce or eliminate, however, is just one part of the process. You also have to know what tasks are important to retain. Now that you know how to better focus, you're ready for the next chapter, which will explain how to identify the high-leverage activities upon which you should concentrate.

Very Important Points

▶ Focus does not come naturally for most people, and that is why it is a skill that must be learned and practiced.

▶ Specifically, focus is a *thinking skill* that is acquired as a result of *mental discipline*.

▶ To develop mental discipline concerning focus, you have to treat it the way you would treat the need for acquiring any skill:

 1. Become aware of the need to improve your focusing skills
 2. Clarify the need, and make a conscious decision to invest the time and energy needed to improve your skills
 3. Focus on the need, and practice and train your mind to focus
 4. Execute the need by implementing your new skills and making them a routine that is second nature

▶ Four strategic facts and characteristics about your behavior confirm your ability to execute and focus at a higher level:

 1. Fewer distractions
 2. More high-leverage activities
 3. On-time performance
 4. Increased productivity

CHAPTER 5

Finding Focus and Producing Real Results

☞ *Fully understanding where you want to go and where you are today will help you locate focus and develop Strategic Leverage.*

Chapter 4 discussed the importance of developing the ability to concentrate on high-leverage activities. When you eliminate distractions and focus on the actions that really matter, you'll more quickly reach your goals and ultimately realize your vision. But now I want you to think of focus not as just something you *do*, but also somewhere you *go*. Focus can also be a location, and when you find it, you will have what I call *strategic leverage*. Strategic leverage is produced when you organize your goals and zero in on the activities that produce real results. This chapter will show you how to locate focus and develop strategic leverage.

Compare Your Current Situation with Your Future Vision

Discovering your high-leverage activities begins by understanding that there are two mental points:

1. Your vision of where you want to be
2. The reality of where you are

Between those two mental points, there is a gap that contains the high-leverage activities, or every strategy, objective, and action step you will need to take to realize your vision. In this gap, you can also locate your focus. Here is a simple graphic that illustrates my point:

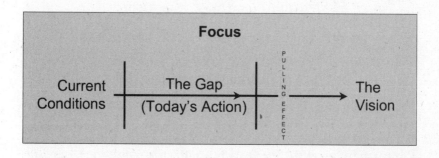

▪ ▪ ▪

As discussed in all the previous chapters, the clarity of your vision generates a pulling effect and empowers you to cross the gap faster and more effectively. This pulling effect is the most powerful and significant benefit of having clarity, but the pulling effect can be diminished if you do not have the proper focus on the most significant things you need to do every day.

Let's return briefly to the story I shared in Chapter 1 about George Burke, the entrepreneur from Atlanta with the successful commercial paint-contracting business. You may recall that George's vision for future growth was challenged by his belief that he had maxed out his time. He erroneously believed he had to be personally involved in a long list of tactical responsibilities to maintain his business's success. And because the things he did personally ate up all his time, he believed he was out of options for future growth. Ultimately he figured out how to solve his time shortage by duplicating himself in others. He accomplished this by finding and training people he trusted, individuals who would sell and manage important contracts with just as much care and concern as he did personally, which made more time available for him.

> **❝Strategic leverage is produced when you organize your goals and zero in on the activities that produce real results.❞**

However, just finding more time was only part of his vision for new growth. By working with me to learn the Strategic Acceleration methodology, George began by creating the goal of adding specific volume opportunities with high profit margins, then identifying high-leverage activities that supported his goal. His high-leverage activities included improving his lead-generation process, pursuing more long-term contractual agreements, investing more in marketing, and maximizing his database of individual and professional contacts. He focused his time and energy on those activities, created strategic leverage, and doubled his revenue.

Can you visualize your activity as an impact gauge that has a needle on it indicating the effectiveness of the action you take? On the far right of the impact gauge is your vision. When the action you take has a direct impact on moving closer to your vision, the gauge needle moves to the right, toward your vision. In contrast, if the action you take does *not* produce results that move you closer to your vision, the needle does not move significantly. High-leverage activities that produce strategic leverage always move the needle to the right, and those are the activities that require your focus.

When you begin to create strategies, objectives, and action steps, you need to evaluate everything you do in relationship to your vision. When you understand that, it makes the need for clarity even more compelling. If you don't have clarity concerning your vision, there will be no standard against which you can evaluate the strategies, objectives, and action steps you create. And without that kind of standard, you will have no way to measure how well any action you take will move the results needle. I have already firmly established the need and the value of clarity, so I don't need to discuss it again. It is important, however, to understand the relevance of vision to your ability to focus on high-leverage activities.

Equally important is the need to have clarity concerning *current conditions*, because *current conditions* establish the launch position for your journey across the gap. You have to know where you are before you can begin to travel to a destination. This may seem obvious, but let's look at an example that shows this isn't as easy as it sounds.

❝*In the end, you're measured not by how much you undertake but by what you finally accomplish.***❞**
—Donald Trump

Let's say your spouse and children come to you and invite you to play a game with them. They tell you only that the game will end by asking you a question you will not be able to answer, although you should be able to answer it. Somewhat confused by all this, you agree to play. They are thrilled that you are willing to play, and they laugh and giggle as they slip a blindfold over your eyes and lead you out to the family car and put you in the backseat. Your "kidnappers" drive you around for a while, and you have no idea where they are taking you.

Then the car stops and you are allowed to get out of the car. When your family removes your blindfold, you find yourself in the middle of the woods, and all you can see are trees. Your captors then say, "Do you know where our house is?" You think, of course you know where your house is because you live there! You leave your house every morning and you return to it at night. You can clearly visualize the location of your house. You say, "Yes, I know where the house is!" You are confident you have won the game, because you were able to answer their question.

Then they ask you to give them specific directions to the house from the spot where you stand. You suddenly realize you have been asked a question you can't answer because you don't know where you are. The location of your house is crystal clear in your mind, but you can't explain how to get there because you do not know where you *are* in relationship to the house.

The point of this story is that having clarity about your vision can't begin to pull you toward it until you know where you are today. Professionally, this might mean that you want a promotion, but because you don't know where you are on the career ladder, you don't know where to put your foot first. The difference between where you are today and where you want to go might be a need for more responsibility, training, or experience, and to move ahead you need to know for sure what is necessary for the promotion you want. Personally, you might want a better relationship with a friend, but until you know where you stand with that friend (how they feel about you), you can't really advance the next level of closeness. Understanding your current position in context to where you are will enable you to change your situation.

Getting Clear on Current Conditions

You must collect two critical categories of information to produce clarity concerning your current condition: *strategic positives* and *strategic negatives*. Exercise 12 in Appendix B will help you identify your strategic positives and strategic negatives, but first let's look at each in more detail.

Know Your Strategic Positives

Strategic positives are the strengths you possess that most powerfully impact your ability to succeed. There are five areas to explore that will help you identify those strengths, described in the following paragraphs.

1. Competitive advantage: This consists of the factors that make you or your company or your products or services unique and determines your market share and overall success. It is a combination of the available resources (intellectual, human, financial, material/physical, etc.) and your organizational capabilities, which combine to form your (or your company's, or your business's) distinctive competencies. Ideally, these distinct competencies form the basis for the value you want to create in your product or service. Examples of resources are:

- **Intellectual:** Patents, trademarks, proprietary knowledge, and unique processes
- **Human:** Talented staff, strong leadership, low turnover, and thorough training

- **Financial**: Brand presence, solid credit, available capital, customer satisfaction, and a positive reputation
- **Material/Physical**: Geographic location, inventory strategies, quality products, and other tangible aspects

The capabilities of your business center on its ability to maximize its time, deploy human resources, and communicate your message.

A great example of an organization that consistently succeeds in maximizing its capabilities is FedEx. Since 1971, it has been the leader in just-in-time delivery services, with a strong reputation, a huge fleet, and a widely recognized series of logos and taglines that all support its vision.

2. History: This factor comprises whatever has produced the foundation of your success. Over time, many things can happen to move you away from those things. It could be that market conditions have changed and the things you used to do are now outdated. Or it may be that changes in leadership have caused your organization to lose sight of what made it great. Being aware of those historical success factors is important, and you need to evaluate their current relevance.

Returning to the FedEx example, the ability to be nimble has been a hallmark of the company's success. It was the first carrier to start using computers to route packages in the late 1970s; it began shipping internationally in the 1980s; it provided tracking to its customers in the 1990s; and in 2003 it acquired Kinko's. All advancements have increased the company's relevancy and customer offerings, ensuring sustainable success.

3. Satisfaction: This comprises the opinions and beliefs your customers *and* employees have about you, your offering, and its value. Customer satisfaction and employee satisfaction are directly related because your employees and associates create customer satisfaction. If your employees and associates do not support and believe in your product or service, neither will your customers. I consider this to be one of the most important building blocks for positive growth.

For example, as a public speaker, I end each event with a satisfaction survey to determine what I did well and what I could improve. As a success coach, I close every session asking participants to consider the strengths and opportunities they discovered during the session. This helps me understand the specific value they received during our time together. And as an employer and mentor, I regularly "huddle" with my staff and colleagues to make sure we're all on track, together, and working toward mutual success and satisfaction.

4. Strategic principles: These are what drive your business, efforts, and long-term success. For example, my primary philosophy in my business is to always provide value that exceeds my customers' expectations. Another is to complete tasks and projects ahead of schedule. And another is to create and sustain a highly consistent brand that reflects the value my customers will receive. These three principles translate into the following actions:

- Providing value by giving my customers access to all of my resources, connections, processes, libraries, and more
- Hiring and partnering with individuals who have specific expertise that will benefit my clients
- Delivering the final product as quickly as possible
- Continually expanding and refining my offerings to have a greater positive impact on my customers' personal and professional lives

All of my strategic principles, and indeed my brand itself, can be summarized as follows: *"Give value: Do more than is expected."*

These are the core principles that have made my business successful through the years.

One of my clients is a manufacturer of construction and mining equipment. I worked with this company to support its human resource efforts across more than twenty-five business units by providing training strategy and presentation delivery expertise, to be cascaded to many of the company's eighty thousand employees. The head of the HR department had this to say:

> Thank you for your commitment, flexibility, and passion for customer delight. You've set a new standard that other service providers must now try to achieve. We truly had a great return on our investment.

You can see that these principles make the difference in winning and losing, and they can create the tipping point in your customer's mind that consistently comes down in your favor.

5. Strategic opportunities: These are roads that have opened up and become apparent by achieving clarity about your vision. These are choices you should pursue that will add value to your product or service, capitalize on your gifts and strengths, and better meet (and exceed!) customers' needs. Sometimes taking these new roads leads you in a completely different direction than you had originally intended, with favorable consequences.

Here's a great example: In 1927, a young married couple started a hot dog and root beer stand called The Hot Shoppe in Washington, D.C. Over the next two decades, they continued to expand their business, opening many more successful stands and restaurants, and offering food services to large organizations. In 1957, when the American highway system opened up the country and car vacations became a way of life, the couple decided to jump on the opportunity and pursued a slightly different direction. They built a motor lodge, or motel, the success of which enabled them, over the next fifty years, to grow exponentially in this new direction.

The couple? J. Willard and Alice Marriott. The company? Marriott International Inc., which in 2007—eighty years after the first hot dog was sold—generated more than fifty thousand reservations per day at nearly three thousand properties in sixty-seven countries, and had revenues of $13 billion. Capitalizing on strengths and changing your vision as the needs of your customers change can indeed open up incredible opportunity.

Know Your Strategic Negatives

Strategic negatives are the factors that most powerfully contribute to failure or less than satisfactory results. There are four areas to consider that will help you identify those negatives, described in the following paragraphs.

1. Employee complaints: These are what have historically impacted employee satisfaction. Every organization has a history of consistent complaints that come from within. Some of the complaints change as the years go by, but some never seem to go away. Various employee surveys through the years have consistently indicated that employee satisfaction is directly related to customer satisfaction and vice versa. Employees want to be proud of their employer and they want to touch customers in a positive way. For that reason, many internal complaints arise when employees do not feel customers are well served. Four issues go to the heart of employee satisfaction, and financial compensation is not one of them. What people want from their jobs and their careers is actually quite simple:

- A personal sense of accomplishment
- The ability to use their best talents every day
- Consistently receiving feedback on how their work is appreciated by leadership
- Real opportunities to learn and develop

Factually understanding how well these four felt needs are met is a significant part of establishing current conditions. If you do not have employee satisfaction, it will impact customer satisfaction at some point. Creating employee and customer satisfaction is a high-leverage activity!

I have a client who is committed to getting clarity on and improving his employee satisfaction levels. He sends out an annual survey that solicits anonymous employee input on matters of vision, performance, growth, morale, synergy, direction, and more. From there, he hosts open "town hall" meetings to facilitate open discussion of specific and pressing complaints, the results of which drive his executive team's performance standards. By drilling down to the bottom, he reshapes the top, and as a result, he has an organization empowered by information.

2. Customer complaints: These expose the current strategic conditions of your enterprise. Nobody enjoys hearing customer complaints, but they are a gold mine of information and contain a wealth of data. It is generally believed that when one customer takes the time to make a complaint, there are many more who have the same complaint but do not take the time to make it. So one complaint may represent scores of customers.

If you evaluate customer complaints over an extended period of time, some will be consistently repeated. Hopefully, your business is such that you have not allowed these recurring complaints to exist over a long period of time. However, it is important that you know the truth of it. Having a handful of consistent, recurring complaints indicates strategic weakness.

Over the years, I've had many clients in the automotive industry, an industry that has historically been shaped by its customers. When a car is purchased through a dealer, which is a franchise, the manufacturer sends the buyer a satisfaction survey. Based on the results, the manufacturer either rewards or corrects its franchise operator and occasionally makes design changes. This process eliminates weaknesses at both the customer service and product levels and helps the manufacturer keep up with its competition.

3. Competitive opinion: This is what your competitors believe are your strategic shortcomings. When you compete with other businesses for a new customer, you can be certain your competition will make a case about why its offering is superior to yours. Your competitors are always looking for your strategic weakness so they can exploit it to their own benefit. You must understand what they believe your strategic weakness to be so you can create an accurate picture of current conditions.

When I help my clients develop their own success strategies, I often facilitate a competitive comparison matrix. My team will begin by researching specific categories (dependent on industry) to help create a benchmark and further understand the competition. From there, I work with the executives and leaders to tap into their expertise and close any gaps. Performing this relatively simple exercise and keeping it updated as the market changes keep an organization focused and aligned on day-to-day decisions.

4. Failure factors: These are the top issues that could cause you to lose whatever you're working for. In the same way that a handful of core principles drives your success, a handful of issues consistently contributes to your failures. Those issues could relate to price, service, or an inability to communicate value or your unique selling position. Whatever the case, there are always reasons for losing, and it is important to identify those causes. This is particularly true when the reasons keep repeating themselves.

Strategically Merging Positives and Negatives: A Case Study

I'd like to share a little bit about one of the large corporations I work with. I can't reveal details about my work with them, but helping them discover their current conditions energized their focus and their ability to gain strategic leverage and reach better results. I recently had the honor and privilege of working with the top leadership of the company's U.S. sales team.

As the sales executives worked their way through the process of establishing their current conditions, they were reminded of some very significant positives. Among those positives was that they have one of the most recognized brands in the world and the dedication of the company's sales force is unmatched by that of any of its competitors. The executives reaffirmed the value of their collective experience and their long and successful history. The company's historical competitive advantage became clear to them and reaffirmed that it still provided a powerful foundation for future success.

As the executives examined their strategic positives and strategic negatives, they:

- Discovered a need to strengthen the connection between the corporate center and the field, improve their support for field representatives and provide them with more effective tools, and reconcile gaps in the sales force's training and habits
- Determined the high-leverage activities that addressed the above needs: facilitating more frequent and homogenous communication between the corporate center and the field, creating better training materials and clearer brochures and product overviews, and equipping the field with enhanced kits that contain everything necessary to sell or recruit
- Focused on the above high-leverage activities, which in turn produced strategic leverage and created better results

Recent field satisfaction surveys show a marked increase in morale and opinions about training, and sales have increased 7 percent in the past quarter. The point of this illustration is to demonstrate that every business needs to evaluate its current conditions regularly. If a company as large and established as my client can benefit from this process, everyone can. Even if your vision is of a personal nature, taking stock of your true reality is critical to properly defining and refining goals that will ultimately support your success.

Venturing into the Gap

Now that you have achieved clarity concerning your vision and your current conditions, it's time to venture into the gap and begin to focus on the action you need to take to move the needle on your results/impact gauge. The gap between current conditions and your future vision is made up of goals that create a mosaic of activity designed to produce predictable results and success.

❝*The gap between current conditions and your future vision is made up of goals that create a mosaic of activity designed to produce predictable results and success.***❞**

It is not my intent to teach the details of goal setting in Strategic Acceleration. Many books have been written on how to set goals, and if you want to learn more about the mechanics of goal setting, there is no shortage of resources to help you. The specific goal-setting formula you choose is not that important because each formula varies only slightly. The "SMART" goal-setting formula probably captures the most significant elements. If you are not familiar with SMART, the essential components are:

1. Your goal must be Specific.
2. You must be able to Measure your progress.
3. Your goal must be something Attainable.
4. Your goal must be Realistic.
5. Your goal must have a Time deadline.

Suppose you're a salesperson who wants to move up the career ladder. This is a worthy ambition, but to achieve it with the SMART system, you need to translate this general ambition into something like this:

> I want to be promoted to sales supervisor [**specific**] by in-
> creasing my annual sales by 30 percent [**measurable**],
> which I believe I can do because I increased my sales this
> year by 20 percent over last year [**attainable**], and I have
> even more ideas on how to find new clients [**realistic**],
> and, therefore, I would like to be considered for promo-
> tion if I meet these goals by the end of this fiscal year
> [**time deadline**].

Now you're ready to discuss your SMART goal with your
boss and see whether he or she agrees that you're on track to
move up.

Most goal-setting processes also recommend that you segment your life into several categories and then create specific
goals within each category. Typically the categories contain
variations of the following categories:

- Family life
- Professional life
- Financial life
- Physical/health life
- Spiritual life

Surprisingly, when we segment our lives into such categories and base our goal setting on those categories, it can actually create a focus problem. Although it is true that our lives
are composed of these many parts, the fact is that our life is
one life. When we organize our goals into categories like
these, it opens the door to the possibility of investing too
much time in activities that don't have much of an impact on
moving the results needle. Human nature is such that we naturally gravitate toward activities we enjoy, rather than activities we would rather avoid or put off. But when you organize

your goals around a *segmented* life, you run the risk of spending more time on one aspect of your life than others. For example, if you take a lot of pleasure in exercise and physical activities, you might spend more time on your physical/health goals than is really necessary.

The reason that goal-setting gurus suggest the life-segmentation method is that we need to live a balanced life. Organizing goals around our life segments theoretically will produce that balance. This is not always the case, however, and I teach a more effective way to organize and manage your goals. The remainder of this chapter describes that method.

Strategies, Objectives, and Action Steps

Strategic Acceleration is based on doing things that will produce superior results faster. And that, as I have previously stated, involves identifying high-leverage activities and focusing on those activities. When we organize our goals in life segments, it is difficult to incorporate a way of thinking that focuses on and differentiates those high-leverage activities. In other words, when we use the life-segmentation formula, all areas of our lives and all goals become equal. For this reason, you should have a way of organizing your goals that will differentiate high-leverage activities and allow you to focus on action that will move the results needle.

A concept embedded in Strategic Acceleration is that you can see only a certain distance into the future, and your activity should be based on how far you can see. The idea is that as you travel, you will be able to see farther—as I described in Chapter 2, in the story of how Albert Mensah achieved his goal of leaving Africa and coming to America by working methodically, one step at a time. The truth of this principle is based on the fact that your life circumstances are unique to your own experience, age, and the felt needs you are attempting to meet.

If you are a single person in your early twenties, how far you can see may be very different from what a forty-year-old married person can see. For example, younger people have a different view of their health needs than older people. Many young people actually opt out of acquiring health insurance because they are not worried about illness. Married people in their forties, however, position health care as a top priority. So going as far as you can see and then being able to see farther relates to your own individual needs and perspectives. Let's look at another, more detailed example.

Putting Value in Perspective at The News Group: A Case Study

One of my customers is a large corporation known as The News Group, a company that distributes books and magazines into retail outlets such as Safeway, Wal-Mart, and just about every airport bookstore in America. The News Group's senior managers hired my company to help them clarify their vision and to develop a new focus for their future.

The company's challenge was to improve its ability to sell based on value, not price. Because the competition in the company's industry was limited to a handful of companies, and because those companies had achieved parity in operational effectiveness, their customers could not differentiate between them with respect to value. Therefore, selling their services had become strictly a matter of price. This forced reductions in margin year after year that threatened profitability and long-term survival. A point was finally reached that demanded the creation of new strategies based on the ability to sell value over price.

To help The News Group achieve clarity about a new vision, we began by interviewing the company's major customers and internal leadership. What we discovered was quite amazing. We learned that enhanced value from its customers' perception would be for The News Group to stock merchandise in neighborhood stores, based on the demographics of each particular neighborhood. The ability to do that would surpass any claims The News Group might make concerning superior operational effectiveness or better procedures.

That discovery sparked a new initiative within The News Group for reforming the company based on value-based strategies rather than cost cutting and operational effectiveness. The result of the company's repositioning was a new vision, whereby the senior managers saw an expanded scope for their business that put them in a true partnership with their customers' goals and needs. They saw the opportunity to become a strategic solution for their customers and transcend being a mere vendor. They restated their vision to become "Partners in Innovative Retail Solutions" with their customers.

I do not want to give the impression that operational effectiveness is not important. Operational effectiveness is critical. However, operational effectiveness must be achieved under an umbrella of value-based strategies. Value-based strategies have the greatest ability to move the results needle and for that reason, strategies must become your top level of focus. Regardless of the nature of your vision, having true perspective and realizing value can create broader opportunities for success through enhanced awareness and strategic repositioning.

Regardless of the nature of your vision, having true perspective and realizing value can create broader opportunities for success through enhanced awareness and strategic repositioning.

Organizing Your Goals and Locating Your Focus at Three Levels

Remember, Strategic Acceleration asks you to focus your time and effort on goals and activities that have a higher probability of moving the results needle. The best way to create and organize your goals to recognize your specific needs and identify high-leverage activities is to create a strategic plan, the development of which is Exercise 13 in Appendix B.

A strategic plan is topped by the **vision**, which is supported by three tiers that will collectively produce the power to propel you across the gap. On the other side of the gap, you'll recall, is the successful realization of the vision. The tiers are composed of different types of goals, some of which create a greater amount of strategic leverage than others:

- **Tier 1—Strategy:** At the first tier are the *strategies* you must develop to execute your vision successfully. These goals will produce the highest degree of strategic leverage. Senior leadership must develop these goals, and it is the tier upon which senior leadership should spend its time and effort.

- **Tier 2—Objectives:** On the second tier are *objectives* that lead to successfully executing your strategies. These goals are more tactical in nature. Leaders at the mid-management level spend their time here. These activities produce strategic leverage, but less than Tier 1 activities.

- **Tier 3—Actions:** Finally, at the third tier you see the *actions*, or specific steps that must be accomplished to successfully reach your objectives. Tier 3 goals produce the lowest amount of strategic leverage, but they must be accomplished to successfully complete the Tier 1 and Tier 2 goals.

To use a military analogy, the relationship of vision, strategy, objectives, and action steps can be understood as the components in a war:

- **Vision** is the highest component and represents the big picture and the end result of successfully conducting the war.
- **Strategies** relate to major campaigns that have to be successfully completed to win the war.
- **Objectives** represent the major battles that must be fought to achieve victory in the strategic campaigns.
- **Actions** represent specific troop and resource allocations that must be made during specific battles.

Differentiating Your Focus at Each Tier of Your Vision

Now I want to discuss the three levels of focus in some detail. It is important that you understand the distinctions that separate and define each level of focus.

- **Strategy (Tier 1):** Strategies represent what you must *become* along the way as you cross the gap to your vision. Strategies are about creating conditions that produce unique, competitive advantages that come together to support the successful execution of your vision. The most important thing to understand about strategies, however, is that they are not really about tactical actions. They are completely strategic. Strategies should relate to *creating value* and *enhancing value* because that is what creates long-term sustainability of your competitive advantage and your success. For that reason, creating relevant strategies is the most significant critical success factor in being able to identify high-leverage activities.

- **Objectives (Tier 2):** The most important thing to re-member about creating Tier 2 objectives is that they must be based on the strategies created in Tier 1. Ob-jectives are specific components of what the strategy must achieve, and they represent the goals that are most critical to achieving those strategies. When you begin to establish objectives, you are beginning to tran-sition into focusing on the action you need to take in the *present*. The strategies created in Tier 1 have more of a *long-term* perspective and represent how far you can see. In contrast, the objectives you create to achieve those strategies represent the more *immediate* tasks you must perform so you can actually go as far as you can see.

- **Actions (Tier 3):** Action steps are mini-objectives made up of the specific things you must do *on a daily and weekly basis*. To guarantee that your action steps lead to the highest level of strategic leverage, you must put them to the same test you used to create strategies and objectives. You have to ask if the action step will have a *direct* impact on helping you successfully complete the objective to which the action step is related. Action steps are the *most immediate* issues you must deal with, and they are always found in the *near* present.

Putting It All Together

I want to share an example of how developing a clear *vision* and supporting it with the three tiers of *strategy, objectives,* and *actions* can create real focus and real results. Terex Cor-poration manufactures heavy equipment used in mining, road construction, utilities, and other infrastructure indus-tries. The company makes a significant investment in show-ing its products at large-equipment trade shows. The cost of organizing the company's presence at these shows is quite high, and the senior managers wanted to be certain that they maximized the benefits of this type of investment by communicating their true value to customers, which of course would result in relationships and sales. They hired me to help them achieve that goal.

- **Vision:** Their vision was as follows, with respect to three areas:
  1. Customers—to be the most customer-responsive company in the industry, as determined by their customers
  2. Financial—to be the most profitable company in the industry, as measured by return on invested capital
  3. Team members—to be the best place to work in the industry, as determined by their team members
- **Strategy:** The strategy we developed for Terex was to increase new opportunities with customers at trade shows.
- **Objectives:** To accomplish this strategy, several specific objectives were established, but the most significant was:

> To create and deploy a powerful training program to be presented in a webinar format prior to major trade shows, to trade-show personnel that would enhance their ability to communicate the value of Terex products to customers.

In this objective, you can see all the elements of "what," "how," "why," and "when" were incorporated into the language of the objective.

- **Actions:** The numerous actions we developed to support the objective included various methods of training their team members and ensuring that they retained what they learned during the training.

Successfully training their trade-show group reached a significant milestone for Terex in that their team members' ability to communicate value to their customers increased significantly. In a letter I received from Kevin Janco, senior director of marketing and branding for Terex, he said:

> We observed a real change in behavior among our team members at ConExpo, which helped make it our best cross-business trade show ever.

The project with Terex helped the senior managers create strategic leverage and the ability to focus on a strategy and an objective that moved their results needle one step closer to their vision.

Your vision could be a major undertaking or something simple yet important to you. Whatever your desired end result, developing a clear vision and supporting it with the three tiers of strategy, objectives, and actions can create real focus and real results.

Summary

Strategic Acceleration provides a method of focus designed to help you get more done faster. The foundation of that idea is strategic leverage, which is gained by being able to focus on activities that move the results needle. Focus is indeed a location between two points, and it is found in the gap between *where you are* and *where you want to go*. The key to getting superior results faster is in concentrating and focusing on actions that really make a difference.

Now that you have clarity and focus, you're ready for the next section of the book, execution, which comprises persuasion, production, and presence. Persuasion is the topic of Chapter 6, which will provide you with the skills to solicit help and buy-in from others who can help you realize your vision.

Very Important Points

▶ Discovering your high-leverage activities begins by understanding that there are two mental points:
   1. Your vision of where you want to be
   2. The reality of where you are

Between those two mental points is a gap that contains the high-leverage activities, or every *strategy*, *objective*, and *action step* you will need to take to realize your vision. In this gap, you also locate your focus.

▶ You must collect two critical categories of information to produce clarity concerning your current condition:
   1. *Strategic positives* are the strengths you possess that most powerfully impact your ability to succeed.
   2. *Strategic negatives* are the factors that most powerfully contribute to failure or less-than-satisfactory results.

▶ A strategic plan is topped by the vision, which is supported by three Focus Tiers that will collectively produce the power to propel you across the gap; on the other side of the gap is the successful realization of the vision.

▶ The three Focus Tiers are:
   Tier 1: The *strategic goals* you must develop to execute your vision successfully
   Tier 2: The *operational goals* or specific objectives that lead you to successfully execute your strategies
   Tier 3: The *action goals,* or specific steps that you must accomplish to successfully reach your objectives

CHAPTER 6

Persuasion Matters

☞ *Clarity enables you to better persuade and communicate, which is the basis for great execution.*

Chapter 5 covered the concept of strategic leverage, or the ability to organize your goals and zero in on activities that produce real results. Now that you've developed clarity about your vision and can focus on what you need to do to reach it, you can begin to solicit help and buy-in from others who can help you execute. This chapter will teach you how to effect voluntary change in others and work together to exceed expectations.

Strategic Acceleration can be compared to a tripod with individual legs for *clarity, focus,* and *execution.*

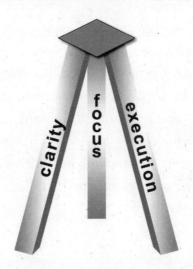

The Strategic Acceleration Tripod

All three legs work together to achieve a common goal, which is to produce superior results faster. As you'll recall from previous chapters, *clarity* is about knowing what you really want and understanding the purpose and value of your vision, and *focus* is about avoiding distractions and learning to identify the high-leverage activities that significantly move the results needle. We have discussed clarity and focus from the perspective of understanding their *core, strategic characteristics*. The next subject, *execution,* must be treated in the same way.

Clarity, focus, and execution are equal parts of the Strategic Acceleration process. None is more important than another, and if you remove one or more of them, you will not be as successful as you want to be. By that, I mean the results you achieve will be less than you need or expect—just as a tripod will fall over if you remove one of the legs. Clarity, focus, and execution are also linked together in a progression or process. Clarity provides the foundation for focus. Clarity and focus together form the basis for execution. Though all three are important, the bulk of your time will be spent on execution. The reason it takes more time than clarity and focus is that execution is about *doing*. Clarity and focus provide a road map and form the *basis* for doing what you need to do, but execution is about *actually doing it*, and this is why it's the most time consuming. As with clarity and focus, there are core issues about execution that are strategic and very important.

Execution also sits on a tripod. Its legs are Persuasion, Production, and Presence.

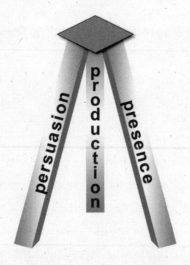

The Execution Tripod

This chapter discusses persuasion, Chapter 7 explores the issue of production, and Chapter 8 deals with presence.

Persuasion Is Critical to Execution

The best way to understand the significance of persuasion and the role it plays in execution is to recognize how much of your time is invested in persuading others. What percentage of your total effort do you spend persuading others—20 percent? 50 percent? More than that? The answer to that question certainly depends on what you do for a living, but if you are a business leader, if you are an entrepreneur, if you are involved in sales, or if you are in any way involved with other people, I can tell you that most of your time is involved in some form of persuasion. Also, if you are married or have children, you are constantly involved in persuasion. If you do any volunteer work, you are always trying to persuade others to support your charity or your project. If you are involved in politics, the entire political process involves persuasion. If you are a pastor, a doctor, or an attorney, you are invested in persuading others to do what is best for themselves.

**❝*The key to successful leadership
today is influence, not authority.*❞**
—Ken Blanchard

Regardless of your role, you are heavily involved in persuasion, which is why persuasion is one of the strategic elements of execution. You need others' assistance and cooperation to be successful, and your ability to persuade has a lot to do with the willingness of others not only to assist you, but also to do so by *exceeding expectations*. When you can persuade others to exceed expectations, you take execution to a higher level and really move the results needle.

Jane, the new marketing director for a prosperous retirement community, is responsible for keeping occupancy levels high. Therefore, she focuses her efforts on exceeding the current residents' expectations and thinking of innovative ways to attract new occupants. After she took over the position, she critically examined the property and assessed its strengths and weaknesses. Because the community had low lease-renewal rates and low occupancy levels, she felt that something needed to change. She solicited anonymous feedback from her residents and found that improving the outdoor common areas, where residents would often gather for coffee, Bible study, or to show off their grandchildren, would add a lot of value to the residents' quality of life. Moreover, it would significantly improve the property's "curb appeal" during prospective tenants' tours.

❝Persuasion is one of the strategic elements of execution.❞

The residents told Jane that they felt the landscaping and pathways were overgrown and badly maintained, the seating areas were dilapidated and unattractive, and navigating with a wheelchair or walker was a challenge. Jane put together a plan to create a pretty, re-landscaped set of common areas linked by pleasant pathways, with good evening lighting, better wheelchair and walker accessibility, comfortable and tough outdoor furniture, and even a small play area for children visitors. Because the property owners were a miserly conglomeration in another state, however, she knew getting budget approval for these renovations would pose a challenge, despite the positive revenue-based results she was certain she'd see.

"How will I get them to see the value of my idea?" she asked me. I suggested that she have as much ammunition as possible when she presented her request. To that end, she spent a few weeks gathering as much supporting material as she could muster. She took photographs of rival communities' common areas and cited their higher occupancy levels. She had prospective tenants complete post-tour questionnaires that provided good insight into what outsiders thought. She convinced a couple of the more outspoken residents to share their candid feedback about the common areas. The tenants were all delighted in this new employee's interest in their lives. After many years of watching their property slowly deteriorate, they were excited to see potential for change and improvement.

After marshaling all her resources and thinking through exactly what she wanted to say, Jane delivered a powerful presentation to the property owners that persuaded them to fund the improvements. Her success delighted the tenants because it showed that she cared, and her innovations made the property more appealing to newcomers. The community now has a four-month waiting list, and Jane is being considered for the executive director position. She exceeded all of the stakeholders' expectations by effectively persuading her tenants to help her persuade her bosses to invest in the community, and everyone saw tremendous success as a result.

Jane's story is a great example of something I've learned over the years:

> The most successful people are able to effectively convince and persuade other people to take action on their behalf.

I have had a lifelong desire to become the best communicator and persuader I could possibly be. I also wanted to help others improve their communication and persuasion skills. When I started pursuing this vision, I did not understand that my desire to become a better communicator was driven by a more fundamental motivation: I love to win, and I hate to fail!

There is a powerful connection between persuasion and execution. Successful people influence others by knowing what they want to say and how they want to say it, and are able to say it in a way that impacts others and spurs them to take action. Realizing this connection permitted me to increase my own persuasion skills and show others that execution depends on the ability to inspire others.

❝*Successful people influence others by knowing what they want to say and how they want to say it, and are able to say it in a way that impacts others and spurs them to take action.***❞**

I have met many very intelligent people who don't appreciate the powerful relationship between the *skill to persuade* and *success*. Frequently, I've seen attitudes that these skills are not important and are subject to improvement only after more important things were taken care of. Dale Carnegie wrote that 85 percent of a person's financial success is related to his or her personality and ability to lead people. I concur with this assessment because leading people is about persuading people to act in specific ways. A vital principle I've learned is this:

When everything else is equal, the ability to effectively present and communicate your ideas is the greatest single factor in success!

I believe this is true because my own success has frequently depended on motivating and persuading others to take positive action on my behalf. Effective communication and presentation skills require you to plan *what* you want to say, and how you will *deliver* that message. An effective delivery will enable you to convince others to take action on your behalf. In Appendix C, which will help you develop your Execution Blueprint, you will learn the 3-D Outline concept (Exercise 14), which describes what you want to say and how you'll say it, and outlines all the actions behind a successful delivery.

Your ability to persuade others has a direct impact on being able to get superior results faster. In Chapters 4 and 5, I emphasized the importance of identifying and focusing on high-leverage activities that have the best chance to significantly move the results needle. However, identifying and focusing on those activities is only the beginning. Once you know what your high-leverage activities are, you face the challenge of actually *doing* them, which usually involves other people. Beyond persuading others to help you, however, you need to persuade them to act quickly. As you begin to execute your high-leverage activities, you will inevitably reach a point where you will be waiting for other people to complete a task or series of tasks before you can complete the activity. When you are waiting, you are burning time! Your ability to persuade people to take action *faster* will directly impact how often and how long you have to wait. To persuade people to move faster, you have to convince them to *exceed expectations*.

What It Means to Exceed Expectations

Throughout this book, I have discussed the importance of voluntary change, which is important in your own behavior as well as in the behavior of others. Chapter 1 discussed this principle at length. When you are ready to execute your vision, you need to create the willingness to exceed expectations, which pivots on your understanding of the dynamic and definition of exceeding expectations.

Through the years, I have learned a lot about meeting and exceeding expectations, and one of the things I've learned is that it's not complicated or hard to understand. Expectations are *met* when things happen the way people expect them to happen. However, *expectations are exceeded when positive things happen that people do not expect.*

❝*Be a yardstick of quality. Some people aren't used to an environment where excellence is expected.*❞
—Steve Jobs

I want to be very clear about why exceeding expectations is the strategic mind-set that leads to the creation of superior results. Exceeding expectations is a strategic way of thinking based on the fact that we ultimately become and do what we think. The mind is the engine of action, and action produces results. Every illustration I've provided in this book reflects this truth. When people have something clear in their minds and it becomes the focus of their thinking, it shapes who they are and all that they do. It is the reason a clear vision has the power to pull us forward until we achieve it. When we understand that our thinking directly translates into results, we can see why thinking in terms of exceeding expectations is so powerful. To persuade others to exceed expectations requires us to be able to persuade them to *think differently about what they do and how they do it.*

When it comes to the role of persuasion in execution (the action we take daily), persuading others to exceed expectations is the most significant. Why? It's because all human beings have expectations about everything in their lives. It is a universal human characteristic. People have expectations about their relationships, their jobs, their families, the cars they drive, the food they eat—the list could go on forever. The point is that every experience we have in life has an expectation attached to it. In the same way, whatever action we take engages either the expectations we have for ourselves, or it engages others' expectations. Therefore, strategically considering how our goals will impact expectations becomes the critical mind-set for creating superior results. Exercise 15 in Appendix C will help you determine how you can exceed expectations. When you are able to surpass your own and others' expectations, Strategic Acceleration begins to flow over to every part of your life and becomes the basis for your ability to get superior results faster.

How Exceeding Expectations Impacts Results

The execution of any vision requires a mix of good planning, the creation of effective strategies, and the establishment of specific objectives and goals. However, you should not jump into these activities without clarity and focus, and you should precede any action you take with some deep thinking about how to exceed expectations in a positive way. Your ability to understand your own and others' expectations can actually create a benchmark description of current conditions. Current conditions usually represent what I call a *neutral expectation,* an expectation that something will happen the way you expect it to happen. Remaining in current conditions will keep producing the same results because your actions and the actions of others won't change. You will keep doing what is expected. Therefore, exceeding expectations in a positive way is the first step in making the departure from current conditions.

Understanding Expectations

Understanding how expectations are created is the first step in being able to exceed them in a positive way. Expectations come from our experience. As our experience changes, our expectations change, too. To illustrate how this happens, I want to share an example. It involves a tool that has changed the way we all work and communicate: voice mail. Prior to voice mail, when you dialed an office phone number, your neutral expectation was to hear a live person answer the phone. When voice mail first appeared, however, that neutral expectation was suddenly shaken by an invitation to leave a personal recorded message. The first time I encountered voice mail, I hung up! It was such a departure from my expectations, I didn't know how to respond to it.

> **❝Your ability to understand your own and others' expectations can actually create a benchmark description of current conditions.❞**

The original intent and strategy of voice mail was to create a positive tool that would exceed expectations by significantly improving the speed and results of telephone communication. Prior to the advent of voice mail, the expectation of callers and callees was to get caught up in a process that can best be described as message-slip phone tag. The message slips were created by switchboard operators and receptionists, who handed the message slips off to the people being called. Typically, the message slips merely reflected the name and number of the caller, and the reason for the call was fairly short and cryptic. Message-slip phone tag was the standard of telephone use until the advent of voice mail.

As with most good ideas, voice mail as it was originally intended accomplished a great positive result. It enabled people to leave personal recorded messages for specific people, who could return their calls more efficiently. Voice mail helped synchronize telephone communication to the real-world work environment. The ability to leave content-rich messages allowed people to engage the purpose of their call much faster and reduce the time it took to resolve problems. Prior to voice mail, only one in four calls made through a switchboard connected in real time to the person being called. Getting a message of content through via message slips was a hit-or-miss proposition. Voice mail allowed callers to leave a message directly with the person they needed 100 percent of the time. Clearly, voice mail exceeded business callers' expectations in a positive way and led the way to superior results, faster.

How times have changed! Today our neutral expectation is to get a voice mail system when we place a call to any size of business. Our collective experience over the past twenty years has completely reversed our expectations about what will happen when we make a phone call. Now we rarely expect people to answer their phone, at their business or at their home! Expectations are always changing, based on experience. This reinforces the need to make exceeding expectations a strategic foundation that precedes action. This is what drives the need to persuade others to embrace the willingness to exceed expectations.

The principle you want to persuade others to accept is this:

> The expectations we exceed
> today become the seed for
> new opportunities in the future.

This may seem to be an obvious fact, but many people fail to connect today's actions with future opportunities. In fact, entire businesses have been built and nurtured around strategies of exceeding expectations. The story of Howard Schultz, the founder of Starbucks Coffee, is a well-known tale of business success, but I want to briefly discuss an aspect of the Starbucks strategy that doesn't get much attention and is a great example of exceeding expectations in a big way. It also presents an example of what can happen when you depart from that strategy.

Howard Schultz's commitment to exceeding expectations permeated everything Starbucks did from the day he acquired the business. Schultz exceeded customers' expectations by creating what he called "a third place." Starbucks worked to create a place people thought of going that was third only to their homes and workplaces. Starbucks created an environment that combined aroma, comfort, friendliness, and a participatory experience of coffee making and coffee drinking. Exceeding the customer's expectation about coffee drinking was at the heart of this environment, and it certainly worked. Starbucks claims its regular customers will frequent one of its stores a staggering eighteen times each month! Starbucks changed America's expectations about coffee drinking to the extent that it changed our culture.

Not only did Schultz exceed the expectations of the coffee-consuming American, but he also exceeded the career expectations of those who typically apply for work in retail food chains. On a CBS *60 Minutes* segment in 2006, Schultz said he was scarred by the memory of his father sitting at home with a cast on his leg with no insurance, and that memory had created a deep commitment to respect his employees. It produced his approach to the Starbucks employment benefit package.

What can most people expect when they apply for a job in a small retail food business? Can they expect employer-provided health care for themselves and their families? Can they expect employer-provided health care for working part time? Can they expect to be able to buy stock in the business?

Well, they can if they apply for a job at Starbucks. Starbucks claims to spend more for employee health care than it does for coffee beans! When you pay $4 for your Starbucks beverage, you are paying for health care, stock options, and more that go to benefit Schultz's employees. Starbucks employees have had their career expectations positively exceeded.

The Starbucks story took another turn in the year 2000 when Schultz stepped down as CEO and moved into the role as chairman of the board of directors. For the next several years, Starbucks's financial performance declined and its stock value began to fall. On February 14, 2007, Schultz sent a memorandum to the senior executives of Starbucks. He was concerned about the way Starbucks was heading and feared the company had lost sight of what had made it successful. He called the problem "The Commoditization of Starbucks." In that memorandum, Schultz said,

> As you prepare for the FY 08 strategic planning process, I want to share some of my thoughts with you. Over the past ten years, in order to achieve the growth, development, and scale necessary to go from less than 1,000 stores to 13,000 stores and beyond, we have had to make a series of decisions that, in retrospect, have lead to the watering down of the Starbucks experience, and, what some might call the commoditization of our brand. Many of these decisions were probably right at the time, and on their own merit would not have created the dilution of the experience; but in this case, the sum is much greater and, unfortunately, much more damaging than the individual pieces.

Schultz went on to talk about specific things they had done that changed the Starbucks experience. He mentioned the equipment they installed that blocked the customers' view of the coffee-making processes. He talked about the loss of coffee aroma that resulted from using airtight bags for their coffee beans and the change in overall store design that had diminished the neighborhood feel of the stores. Schultz asserted that these and other factors had changed the Starbucks environment from the original concept of Starbucks as a "third place" and were at the root of current problems. They had stopped exceeding the expectations of their customers, and they were not even meeting them.

Once Starbucks changed the coffee-consumption culture in America by changing expectations, the company forgot that the change would eventually revert back to being the status quo. When the company began to make other changes that eroded the "third place" environment, it was actually exceeding expectations again, but in a negative way. Over time, it began to impact financial performance.

In January 2008, Schultz reclaimed the CEO position at Starbucks and committed himself to getting the company back on track. In April 2008, he was interviewed for *BusinessWeek* magazine by Maria Bartiromo. While sharing his strategy to reestablish the Starbucks image and growth, Schultz said,

> But the job of every retailer and every merchant is to put yourself in the shoes of the customer and ask yourself: "Are you exceeding their expectations?" That's what we have to do as a business.

Schultz was clear in this interview that he was going to return to the core principles that had differentiated Starbucks from the beginning. He intended to return to his primary strategy of exceeding customer expectations.

Persuasion Is the Key to Exceeding Expectations

The Starbucks story is a great example of how exceeding expectations can create and sustain tremendous success for a business. By persuading his retailers and merchants to think like their customers, he was able to recapture the mind-set of exceeding expectations, which ultimately allowed Starbucks to return to its core strategic principles.

However, there is more to exceeding expectations than merely adopting it as a global business strategy. Exceeding expectations has its greatest impact when it is adopted by individuals as a way of life. When you have a group of people who are all willing to exceed expectations in the normal course of their daily activity, you have created a powerful force for superior results. The results produced are achieved faster and of a better quality.

It is rare for anyone to exceed expectations unless they do it on purpose. To *exceed expectations on purpose* means you have an understanding of expected performance, and you realize that expected performance is in no way extraordinary. It becomes tougher when you realize that exceeding expectations requires more effort to surpass what might be described as "acceptable performance." Acceptable performance is in fact mediocrity, and mediocrity is usually the norm. Excellence is not something that is routinely expected; therefore, exceeding expectations always produces excellence.

Every human being is capable of producing excellence, because every human being is capable of exceeding expectations. The only thing that has to happen to *regularly produce excellence* is to become willing to *regularly exceed expectations*. As simple as it sounds, most people do not become willing to practice excellence on a daily basis until they are persuaded to do so.

> An essential function of leadership is to
> persuade and motivate others to pursue
> excellence by helping them become
> willing to exceed expectations.

The Three Elements of Effective Persuasion

Persuasion is the cornerstone of great execution. Now you need to develop the understanding of what it takes to become a more effective persuader. There are two ways to address that issue. One way would be to have a lengthy discussion of specific communication and presentation skills you could practice. That approach, however, would not address the strategic challenge of persuasion. It is not that tactical skills are not important, because they are very important. In fact, I've written more than a dozen books on this very topic (they are all available at www.tonyjeary.com). The second way, the Strategic Acceleration process, concerns itself with your vision's "why" and purpose and explains the thinking you need to embrace to accomplish it. Persuasion is no different. There are three strategic elements in persuasion you must clearly understand. These elements not only represent *why and what* you communicate, but they also reflect the *effect* of that communication. So let's take a look at the three elements of effective persuasion.

Persuasion Element 1: Communicate at the Belief Level and Explain the "Why"

The importance of persuasion became vividly clear to me in the late 1980s when I spent some time as a national speaker for a seminar promotion group. I traveled to a new city each week and delivered a key presentation to a captive audience. The purpose of the presentation was to get the audience to take some specific action. Apparently I wasn't very good at giving these presentations, and that was a rude awakening for me.

After each presentation, my promoters would escort me up to a hotel room and tell me everything I did wrong. Without fail, they always had a long and humiliating list of every error I committed: I slouched, I mumbled, I fidgeted with my hands and forgot to spit out my gum. I bored everyone in the room, including myself, and often got lost in my own stories. My examples weren't relevant, I had an annoying fondness for saying "um" almost continuously, and I was easily sidetracked by people yawning or looking at their watches, which happened frequently. In fact, during one particularly terrible presentation, I called for a break, and fewer than half the participants returned! Realizing that my audience fled to the restroom to free themselves from my presentation torture was sobering, to say the least.

My postsession feedback surveys said I was "too salesy, unbelievable, and didn't seem to know the topic." And the action the participants were supposed to take after enduring one of my sessions? Not only was I failing to persuade others of the value of the action, but I also often completely forgot to reinforce that call to action. This wasted the time and money of everyone concerned, and my promoters were threatening to fire me. I didn't believe in myself, my audience didn't believe in me or my message, and my promoters suggested I try any other line of work I could think of. Instead of giving up, however, I decided to truly commit to improving my skills and exceeding my promoters' expectations.

I critically examined the reasons behind my failure. I was not clearly explaining the "why" behind my calls to action, I did not fully believe in my message, and I lacked confidence. I vividly remember standing in front of a room and witnessing the boredom of the poor souls who had chosen to come hear me speak. One woman was folding origami cranes out of my printed agenda. A four-person table in the back was involved in a heated Hangman tournament. At least six people were snoozing, and one guy would intermittently snore so loud that he'd startle everyone around him—but at least it was a break in the monotony. The people who were tuned in looked slightly horrified at my ineptitude, except for the gentleman right in the middle of the room who would occasionally laugh at my blunders. Looking back, I'm sort of amazed that I wasn't pelted with balled-up paper and cookies from the afternoon snack tray.

It was obvious I would have to study and work hard to learn how to persuade my audiences to take the action I wanted them to take. I eventually saw that to produce voluntary change, I would have to better know what I wanted to say and how I'd say it, and then deliver my message in an impactful, inspiring way that authentically explained the "why." I began to really think through what would influence my audience to take the action my promoters wanted them to take, and I started to experiment with different presentation techniques. I got some books by the experts of the day, and I watched videos of the speakers I admired. I used a stronger voice, made powerful pauses, and carried myself with confidence. I would occasionally ask questions "out of the blue" to keep audience members on their feet. I incorporated small-group exercises or polls that would strengthen my points and set them up for the eventual call to action. I walked around more, I used verbal hooks and cues that reinforced my main message, and without being repetitive, I "told them what I was going to tell them, I told them, and I told them what I told them"—all while reminding them of the "why" in a truthful and authentic way.

It took some time, but after I spent a few months really focusing on and changing what made me a terrible presenter, and learning from others who had a lot to teach me, my promoters no longer wanted to fire me on the spot. In fact, they were quite pleased with both my improvement and the results I was getting. I learned how to present myself and my message authentically, change my audience's beliefs, and persuade them to take the desired action. I was creating voluntary change.

In previous chapters, I discussed the importance of voluntary change. You must remember that the purpose of persuasion is to ultimately change other people's attitudes and behaviors. To produce this kind of change, you must impact people at the level of belief because people become willing to change voluntarily only when they change what they believe. Nothing has a greater impact on what people believe than the perception that they are being told the truth.

Great leaders are not afraid to tell the truth, even if it hurts. If there is a golden rule of persuasive communication it is this: *Don't* mislead others! One of the large problems in business is the corporate rumor mill and the back-channel gossip that materially impacts employee attitudes and behavior. The negative spin this phenomenon generates is usually the result of distorted perceptions about what is really going on, and when that happens, false perception becomes reality.

Communicating at the level of belief involves a heavy dose of "why" being constantly explained. "Why" is communicated by explaining value and purpose, the very items you so diligently pursued in the process of gaining clarity about your vision. The same characteristics that caused *you* to believe in your vision will cause *others* to believe in it as well. Communicate the "why" to create buy-in.

Persuasion Element 2: Set a Powerful Example by Your Own Behavior

Jack Welch is the legendary retired CEO of General Electric. Welch lived by the principle of setting an example of the behavior he hoped to reproduce in his team. Welch wanted to persuade his associates to be energetic and to inspire others to be energetic. Welch himself constantly displayed energy in his own behavior and translated that energy into the ability to execute. Welch was an expert at using communication and motivation to demonstrate his own energy. Welch proactively looked for ways to make his presence felt. He made a regular practice of sending handwritten notes not only to the people who reported directly to him, but also to hourly workers throughout GE. He wrote the intimate and spontaneous notes with his black felt-tip pen on his chairman's stationery. The moment he finished the note, it was faxed to the recipient and the original would soon be in that person's hands. By doing this he was able to demonstrate his willingness and commitment to invest his personal energy in those he needed to persuade to follow his example.

Welch desired his team to possess many other characteristics, and if he had not demonstrated those traits in his own behavior, he would not be worthy of the acclaim he enjoys today. Welch's greatest achievement as a leader was to persuade a team of almost 300,000 people to voluntarily change their behavior to move forward in the same direction with an equal amount of enthusiasm for the purpose of exceeding expectations. In the seventeen years he ran GE, Welch presided with astounding success as peer CEOs dropped like flies in other corporations. He led GE to one revenue-earnings record after another. Noel Tichy, a longtime GE observer and University of Michigan management professor, said of Welch, "The two greatest corporate leaders of this century are Alfred Sloan of

General Motors and Jack Welch of GE. And Welch would be the greater of the two because he set a new, contemporary paradigm for the corporation that is the model for the twenty-first century." The paradigm Welch established was based on persuasion and example.

Have you ever heard the expression "What you do speaks so loud I can't hear what you say!" That remark is a famous quote of Ralph Waldo Emerson, the American essayist, philosopher, and poet who lived in the mid-nineteenth century. Emerson's observation was true in 1850, and it remains true today. Only 7 percent of communication and persuasion is oral. The other 93 percent is the result of what people see and sense based on tone and other nonverbal clues. So if you hope to persuade others to help you and you do things that involve their willingness to exceed expectations, it will be important that you make a practice of exceeding expectations yourself. Nothing persuades more effectively than a leader who sets the right example for his team, children, associates, and colleagues to follow.

Persuasion Element 3: Demonstrate Confidence in What You Say and Do

Rebecca is an associate creative director for a leading advertising agency. Specifically, she works in the business development department and is part of the team responsible for the creative aspects of proposals and pitches delivered to potential new clients. Each new client represents several hundred thousand dollars in revenue for the agency, so the ideas presented in the proposals need to be unique and powerful.

During the initial brainstorming phase of the proposal development process, she worked with others on the creative team to come up with new ideas and concepts. Some ideas would be used, and some would be discarded. Brainstorming is a collaborative exercise, and she often found that her ideas were not getting attention from others and ultimately being excluded from pitches. This was impacting her reputation as a cutting-edge thinker, something that's vital for long-term success in advertising—especially when the firm's revenues are in question. Her ideas were sound and innovative, so what was the problem?

I sat in as an observer during one of the brainstorm sessions. It was a circus of strong personalities, fast talking, and quick thinking! As the other creatives threw around ideas and animatedly explored options, Rebecca sat quietly on the sidelines, clenching her hands and looking visibly tense. Her attempts to break into the conversation were generally ignored, and when she did get the floor, she prefaced each idea with "Sorry to interrupt," "You've probably already thought of this," or "I don't know if this is what the client wants, but . . ." She knew perfectly well that her ideas were new and exciting, but she didn't want to seem arrogant or pushy. As a result, the stronger personalities and louder voices shaped the pitch and diminished her personal involvement and success.

We worked on developing more confidence, both through body language and verbal cues. She stopped introducing her ideas with apologies, and she learned to use a stronger voice. She began to more fully believe in what she had to offer and made others listen. Although not every idea she presents is accepted for each pitch, she gets consideration and respect, and she has done much to shape several winning pitches. Her manager has suggested she be promoted to creative director due to the innovative ideas she has contributed, many of which clients have used. Specifically, she had the idea to cross-market a client's toothpaste brand with a highly watched reality television show, and solicit audience ideas for new flavors via an online survey. This idea increased exposure of the brand as well as the television show, both of which shared a target audience that found the idea fun. The success of this idea resulted in more viewership for the broadcaster and increased the client's market share.

The ability to present yourself, your requests, and even your vision with confidence is another nonverbal piece of the persuasion formula. Why? Well, it's because of the perception that confident people know what they are doing and can be trusted. Confidence is a natural by-product of certainty.

If you do all the things I suggested in previous chapters to achieve clarity and focus, you will be filled with certainty about your vision, and others will perceive that certainty as confidence. Confidence is produced by understanding your vision's "why," value, and purpose.

There is one other unique key I'd like to share with you relating to confidence. It is difficult for many people to do, but having the ability to *speak with authority* about what you want to persuade others to do is a strong confidence builder. People read a lot of meaning into what you say as well as what you *don't* say. You may be frequently tempted to give a less-than-assertive opinion for the purpose of not appearing arrogant. Those are valid concerns, and there is a correct time and a place for them. When you want to persuade people to do something that involves their making a voluntary change in their behavior, confidence is a more powerful perception than humility. When you say things like "I still have a lot to learn about this" or "You probably know more about this than I do," you are unwittingly sabotaging your own perceived confidence. People want confident leaders who know what they are doing.

Remember, *it's your vision, and you own it!* You understand its value and purpose, and you know what it will take to execute it. Be confident in what you ask others to do.

Summary

As you pursue your vision and its execution, you often will need to rely on other people for help. Your ability to communicate the authenticity of your vision (its purpose and value) directly affects your ability to persuade others to voluntarily and wholeheartedly assist you. Beyond simply getting help, however, you need to inspire others to exceed expectations, which happens when you inspire them to be pulled toward realizing and achieving your vision. Having the ability to present your vision honestly and clearly is the key to creating this voluntary change.

The next chapter will discuss the second leg of the execution tripod: *production*. Production is the completion of tasks and projects in reduced time frames, and it is greatly accelerated by a concept described in Chapter 7 that will allow you to manage the aspects in parallel, adjust the project as you progress, and reach greater results.

Very Important Points

▶ Clarity, focus, and execution are equal parts of the Strategic Acceleration process. Clarity and focus together form the basis for execution. Though all three are important, the bulk of your time will be spent on execution because execution is about *doing*. Clarity and focus provide a road map and form the basis for doing what you *need* to do, but execution is about actually *doing* it, and that is why it's the most time consuming.

▶ Regardless of your role or vision, you need others' assistance and cooperation to be successful, and your ability to persuade has a lot to do with others' willingness not only to assist you, but also to *exceed expectations*. When you can persuade others to exceed expectations, you take execution to a higher level and really move the results needle.

▶ The most successful people can effectively convince and persuade other people to take action on their behalf. They do it by knowing what they want to say and how they want to say it. Then they can say it in a way that impacts others and spurs them to take action.

CHAPTER 7

Production Before Perfection

☞ *To avoid procrastination and get faster results, focus on starting instead of finishing, then adjust as you go.*

In Chapter 6, I discussed the first leg of the execution tripod: persuasion. Your vision's success hinges on your ability to inspire others to effect voluntary change and exceed expectations while helping you reach your goals. Authentically communicating your vision's purpose and value is effective persuasion, which sets you up for the second leg of the execution tripod: production.

Production can be defined as completing tasks and projects in reduced time frames. Obviously, if you can get more work done in less time, you will see results much faster. Of the things you can actually control about your production, one habit has more impact on delaying results than any other: *procrastination*. We all are guilty of procrastination to some extent. There are two kinds:

1. Positive procrastination: This is when you legitimately need some "mental percolation" time to gather your thoughts and get clear on what you need to do.

2. Negative procrastination: This is based on some pretty flimsy excuses to avoid doing something, which will ultimately affect your results in negative ways.

Whereas positive procrastination can be beneficial, you need to overcome negative procrastination to be more effective and finish things faster. My concept of Production Before Perfection (PBP), described in this chapter, is the solution to negative procrastination and the catalyst for great results. Once you understand PBP, you will be astounded by the results you see.

> **"***Every business, job and productive project will have its difficulties, taxing responsibilities and unpleasant aspects. Pressing on and overcoming those factors is where much of the feeling of accomplishment comes from.***"**
> —Darren Hardy, publisher
> of *SUCCESS Magazine*

You can't produce results until you start doing something. If you do nothing, that is exactly what you will get—nothing! Over the past twenty-five years, I have developed a way of working that has enabled me to accomplish more than I ever imagined possible. My approach to managing tasks and projects is centered on my PBP concept, which is a powerful antidote for negative procrastination and perhaps the most significant strategy I use daily. PBP is based on a simple premise:

> You don't have to have all the facts
> and details about something before
> you can start working on it!

Before I tell you more about how to deploy this strategy, however, I need to warn you: *When you begin to practice PBP, you will be doing things in a way that conflicts with the thinking of 90 percent of the people on this planet, and you will encounter resistance.* PBP is not a natural thing for people to do, and you will hear many objections about why you should wait to do something. Waiting and Strategic Acceleration are not compatible. When you wait, you are burning time you will never recover. PBP can be difficult to implement because it requires a lot of voluntary change, even if the change eliminates actions that don't work. You must be persistent and persuasive to inspire others to buy into the PBP concept, and that hinges on the lessons learned in Chapter 6.

❝You must be persistent and persuasive to inspire others to buy into the PBP concept.❞

Not long ago, I was watching *Finding Nemo* with my youngest daughter. This is the animated movie about Nemo, a little fish who gets lost and is pursued by his father, Marlin, with the help of his friend Dory. Near the end, when son and father are reunited, Dory is suddenly swept up with hundreds of other fish in a big trawling net. Although Dory is too large to swim through the net, Nemo is able to join her and the other fish, and he attempts to tell them what to do to free themselves. Marlin panics because he feels his son is in danger, but Nemo persuades him that he can help the trapped fish, most notably Dory, and Marlin relents. Nemo further persuades his father to help tell the netted fish what to do, so as Nemo circulates within the net, his father circulates outside, and together they persuade the fish to "swim down" en masse. At first there is just chaos and panic, but eventually the fish begin to listen to and believe in Nemo and Marlin, and they swim down. The net begins to move toward the ocean floor, rather than toward the boat. The combined weight and pressure of the net full of fish swimming in the opposite direction of the boat causes the winch to seize and break, which in turn drops the net and frees the fish.

This example captures the difficulty of persuading others to change their behavior, but it also shows the power of change. The weight of one little fish was negligible when compared to the huge weight of a fishing boat, but when they combined belief and effort, the fish were able to triumph together. Had they waited, they would have been dumped on the deck and flash frozen for our cooking convenience. But because they acted when they needed to act, because the persuasion was strong enough to influence action, their lives were spared.

The Procrastination Problem

The idea that everything has to be perfect before you can move forward can be used to support and justify procrastination. The main idea of PBP is this: Act first, and get it perfect later! I'm going to give you some specific techniques that will help you begin to practice PBP, but first I want to discuss the problem of procrastination.

No human characteristic restricts results and effectiveness more than procrastination. If you want to accelerate results, there is no room in your life or your business for negative procrastination. Show me a person who consistently fails to get superior results, and I'll show you a person who procrasti-nates a lot. However, that person probably won't *think* of himself as a procrastinator because he has lots of seemingly good reasons for not doing things *today*. Procrastinators are experts at justifying inaction and can convince even the most dubious observers that the best strategy for today is to wait.

I don't want to come down too hard on procrastinators because they have developed their procrastination skills over a long period of time. Do you remember our discussions of the belief window in the early chapters of this book? Well, procrastinators really believe the excuses they have for not doing things today are completely valid. And because they believe their excuses are real, their procrastination is the re-sult of incorrect thinking and an erroneous belief that some-thing is true. Most procrastinators don't *believe* they are procrastinating; they think they are being prudent and cau-tious, which helps them do a better job when they finally get around to doing it.

By nature, I'm an impatient person. Though I may some-times drive my team crazy, I actually think it's a positive characteristic because it leads me to do things now. I live a life of PBP! Sometimes, however, I need to be strategic and manage my impatience. I have to will myself to be patient and let things flow, mature, and roll out. *Strategic impatience* is the ability to manage one's patience to ensure that it does not affect execution by becoming procrastination. Instead, it should be used as a tool to motivate you to take action and get things done.

Identifying the Foundations of Procrastination

You may find some of the following statements familiar. You probably have either heard them from other people, or you may have even believed one or more of them yourself. If you feel a personal kinship with these statements, I suggest that you give serious thought to the possibility that *you* are a procrastinator. Here are five statements that lay the foundation for procrastination.

■ ■ ■

1. "I can do it tomorrow."

This may be the most popular and frequently used justification for procrastination. The reason it's so popular is that tomorrow sounds so close to today. Waiting until tomorrow just doesn't seem like that big a deal. Waiting just one more day won't upset too many people, and there surely are many good reasons that can be created to justify the delay. The weather will probably be better tomorrow. You'll probably be more rested tomorrow and will do a better job. Besides, you probably have something else you need to do today that's more important. This list could go on forever, but I think you get the point. When one person decides to put something off until tomorrow, it may force others to do the same, because they will have to wait on you to finish—and if everyone waits until tomorrow to accomplish his or her own piece of the project, all those tomorrows can actually add up to many, many days that your project will be late. The cumulative effect of waiting until tomorrow can have a dramatic impact on results.

My friend Emma is a highly qualified project manager, but she has an aversion to talking on the telephone. Due to her very slight stutter, she prefers to rehearse and think through any conversation she needs to have. She also likes to write an outline of bullet points that will help her stay on track and remain focused. She freely admits that this ritual of practice and documentation is time consuming and probably just a way to delay what she really does not want to do: talk on the telephone, and perhaps have the person on the other end detect her stutter. She is afraid of looking stupid. I asked her if she would question the intelligence of someone with a slight stutter, and she said, "Of course not! But you never know what other people might think." Emma is limiting her productivity by overthinking unimportant details and not believing in her own capabilities.

❝The cumulative effect of waiting until tomorrow can have a dramatic impact on results.❞

Although this habit of overpreparing is not usually a terrible aspect of her life and is ordinarily just an inconvenience to herself, it recently had a huge effect on her success. After a series of exceptional interviews for a new position with a great company, a position that would have propelled her career and increased her income, she received a phone call from the prospective employer. Rather than call him back immediately, she took a day to think through what he might ask her, what she would say in return, and how she would handle unexpected questions. By then it was Friday afternoon, so she decided to wait until Monday. "He'll just be busy on a Friday afternoon," she thought. When she finally got up the courage to call him, on Monday around lunchtime, she was crushed to hear the following: "Well, Emma, I took the lack of a return phone call as a lack of interest in the position. Just this morning, I offered the position to the candidate who was our second choice." Her procrastination cost her a job—and is a regret she thinks about a lot.

On the upside, though, she has learned to force herself to be more timely with phone calls and less judgmental about her perceived flaws. She now makes all return phone calls first thing in the morning, before enjoying coffee or checking e-mail, and she has increased her productivity and confidence as a result. Maybe she won't miss out on the next job offer.

Waiting until tomorrow is a simple dodge to delay action. The problem with doing it tomorrow is that tomorrow is always one more day away. In my experience, it seems that every new day brings with it a new batch of opportunities and things to do. If we are bogged down in completing yesterday's work, we take ourselves out of the running for today's opportunity.

2. "I don't have everything I need, so I'll wait."

This is a very popular statement used to justify inaction and waiting. It is most often an excuse that salespeople use to avoid making telephone calls to prospects. Have you ever heard any of the following statements?

- "I can't call Frank until I have our new marketing brochure."
- "I can't write the press release until the new product line is announced."
- "I can't think through the next quarter's inventory requirements until I find out about the new pricing policy."
- "I can't respond to Sam's e-mail until I have all the answers to his questions."

There are so many things you can wait for to put off taking action that it is possible to *never* have to do anything again for your entire life! Some people actually try to do just that and suffer frequent career changes because of it. The truth is that you can always take *some* kind of action, regardless of the list of things you think you need before you can start. All you have to do is be honest about it and look for what you can do today. Do not wait until you have everything you think you need before you start doing things.

Another way to think about the above statements might be:

- "Even though I don't have our new marketing brochure, I know it will be ready sometime this week. So I'll call and remind Frank that it's about time for him to place his order, mention that we have some great new marketing materials for him to review, and set up a lunch appointment for next week."

- "Although the new product line hasn't been announced, I have written so many press releases that I can draft it for now, leaving space for the product line specifics. Once I get them, it will be a five-minute addition, and then I can send it out right away."

- "Although the new pricing policy is important, I'm still going to need inventory for the next quarter, so I'll go ahead and look through the last quarter's reports and forecast based on need versus expense, for now. I'll at least have a foundation to work with once the policy is completed."

- "I may not have all of the answers to Sam's questions, but I'll drop him a quick note and let him know that I'm working on them and will have a better response by the end of the week. He'll feel reassured that I am not ignoring him, and this allows me to prioritize my tasks."

When working in parallel progress, none of the elements will be 100 percent perfect. However, most of the time they are closer to perfection than not, and the time, effort, and resources required to incorporate the things needed to make them perfect—little tweaks and modifications—were minuscule compared to the normal process of months. The point is this: *Even if you don't think you have everything you need, start anyway.* If you need to fix something later, you will have the time to do it, and you will be much farther along in your project than you would have been if you had waited.

3. "I can't do it perfectly, so I'll wait."

This excuse doesn't make much sense if you ask yourself the question: Can we ever do *anything* perfectly? I think not. How do you feel about this one? Do you feel as though you have to be able to perform perfectly before you can be willing to act? If you do have this attitude, you are in serious trouble, because you will *never* be able to do anything perfectly.

Another variation of the perfection ploy is this: "I need to do more research until I have all that I need." This excuse is effective because who can criticize anyone for doing research to achieve perfection? A good procrastinator who is skilled in research can present the illusion of productivity without actually being productive. My personal opinion is that you frequently don't know what you will actually need until you start doing something. I find that doing things exposes specific things you really need that you could not have planned for even if you had waited.

I work with a very successful and talented editor of business books who had this to say: "I was often guilty of procrastinating by over-researching. When I was interested in pursuing some business person to write a book, I would try to find out everything about that person. (This was before Google made that easy!) But what I really should have done was just pick up the phone or write a great pitch letter, saying, 'I read the article about you in today's *New York Times* (or this week's *Business Week*), and I'm intrigued by the management approaches you described. I wonder if you've considered writing a book . . .' and *then* find out everything I needed to know about that person in order to convince my colleagues that this CEO or manager would make a great author with a compelling story to tell."

By focusing on *action* instead of all the *details* that really didn't add much to the beginning of the book-acquisition process, she was able to get to the heart of the matter ("You have a compelling story; would you want to write a book?") and eliminate wasted time. She often persuaded those CEOs to work with her because she had called them right away, in-stead of waiting—i.e., procrastinating—until she knew every-thing about them and could make the "perfect" pitch. Often the first call is the best call.

4. "I don't have time right now."

I recognize that some things require more time to com-plete than you think you may have at any particular moment, the reality of which makes this excuse so popular. Why and how do we get the idea that we have to be able to *finish* some-thing before we can work on it? Let me again use a book-writing example to show you what I mean.

A nonfiction book is a collection of chapters. Each chap-ter is a collection of ideas about a specific topic. Each idea may have many subpoints. When I begin a book project, how many books would I complete if I believed I had to finish the entire book in one continuous work session? The answer is that I would *never* complete any book project if I believed this was necessary.

In fact, how many *chapters* of a book would I complete if I believed I had to write a complete chapter in one work ses-sion? I can tell you that very few chapters would ever be started if I bought into that idea. In the same way, how many ideas in a chapter would I complete if I thought I had to fully develop every point of an idea in a single work session? I think you can see the point I'm making.

Sometimes, if I have only a brief amount of time available, I might write only a few sentences or a couple of paragraphs. But the sentences and the paragraphs add up and turn into chapters and, eventually, a book. Having a short amount of time is not a valid reason for not doing something. If you have thirty minutes now, then you can do thirty minutes of work that you won't have to do later. The result is that you will complete projects more quickly and you will not fall victim to procrastination. So ignore your watch and do what you can, when you can. The results will speak for themselves.

5. "Someone else can do it better."

I believe this final excuse represents a lack of confidence. This excuse is a silent one that people make to themselves privately. Some authors and psychologists say procrastination is rooted in the fear of success. I'm not a psychologist, but I think it's more likely people fear *failure* more than they fear success. Let's face it—people don't want to look bad, and they are hesitant to put themselves in a position where they might fail. Procrastination is a tool many people use because they falsely believe it will save them from failure. The truth is that procrastination usually *guarantees* failure.

How many times have you noticed something that needed to be done, or something that could be improved, yet you decided to let someone else do it because you were unsure of your ability to do it? How many times have you had what you thought was a great idea and failed to take action because you believed somebody else could do it better? I think we all have experienced these situations and failed to take action on things that would have been good opportunities for us.

Martin, a financial adviser with a major firm, specializes in creating smart retirement strategies for his wealthy clients. After a year of conducting interviews and meetings with his clients about what they wanted out of their funds, he realized that most people didn't really understand the basics of investing, trusts, taxes, etc. On the other hand, most of the literature and documentation available to the public is dry, complicated, and academic in nature. He thought that creating a simple handbook that was essentially a "Retirement 101" manual would be appealing and of value to his clients. In fact, he mentioned it to several of them, all of whom expressed interest in a tool that would streamline and better explain what they could expect during the process. But Martin was stuck. He wasn't a writer; he wasn't a trainer. He was a financial adviser!

He was worried that the end result would be terrible, unreadable, or useless. "Someone else with a more appropriate background could do a better job," he thought. During this time, one of his clients moved to another city and connected there with an adviser at another branch of the same firm. This client mentioned Martin's handbook idea, and even though this adviser had no writing or training experience, he drafted a user-friendly manual and passed it on to his vice president. The idea was a huge hit and was passed on to the internal training department for modifications and branding. The adviser who didn't sit on the idea got all the credit for Martin's idea, created a valuable tool, and elevated his reputation of being proactive and forward-thinking.

And although you would expect Martin to be embittered by his colleague's success, he instead decided to work with his colleague to develop more client education tools, and now they both regularly collaborate on creating innovative materials. Their latest offering is an interactive forecasting dashboard that permits clients to tweak and modify their portfolios and see expected future results in a simple graphic format, and they are exploring investment opportunities to deploy the dashboard on handheld devices and smart phones. Martin might have missed out on the first wave, but fortunately, he was savvy enough to not let another opportunity pass him by. He, too, is sharing in the success that comes from exceeding expectations.

If you see something that needs to be done and you have the opportunity to do it, don't let someone else seize the opportunity. Be bold and step up to the task. If you are the *first person* to see that something needs to be done, you are probably the *best person* to do it.

❝*If you are the* first person *to see that something needs to be done, you are probably the* best person *to do it.*❞

Procrastination Is Just a Bad Habit!

Procrastination may be many things, but mostly it's a bad habit. Someone once said, "Repetition strengthens and confirms." Simply put, this means that the more you do something, the easier it gets. I believe people learn how to procrastinate over a long period of time, and the more they do it, the easier it becomes. When you practice a habit for many years, it becomes second nature to you, a negative application of the fourth rung of the Effectiveness Ladder, discussed in Chapter 4. You practice the habit on a subconscious level, and it is not the result of a conscious, positive decision. It's just a knee-jerk reaction that seems to have a life of its own.

Habits take time to form, and once they are formed, they are extremely difficult to break. It makes no difference whether the habit is positive or negative. A habit is a habit. Positive habits can become as natural for you as bad habits. If you are in the habit of saying "thank you," it is something you do naturally and spontaneously. If you are in the habit of exercising daily, it becomes a part of your routine. The longer you exercise, the easier it becomes. If you develop the habit of looking for *opportunities* rather than looking for *failure*, you will do it naturally. It will become a habit.

I'm not an advocate of complicating things. I believe the best solutions are usually simple, and when we overthink problems, we can make them more complicated than they should be. Lots of people wallow around in their problems for a long time. It's almost as though they are procrastinating on improving their own well-being by overcomplicating what they need to do to fix the problem in question. I believe that habitual problems are easy to identify and that solutions to those problems are usually fairly simple. If you are in the habit of doing something destructive, you have learned that behavior by repetition. If you want to break a destructive habit, you have to practice opposite behaviors long enough to allow them to replace the destructive ones. There is a pop culture saying that goes like this:

> You can think your way into
> bad action, but you can act
> your way into right thinking.

This statement frames the issue perfectly.

Unfortunately, people are very protective of their bad habits. They almost seem to think they are beneficial, and there is a fear of letting them go. I've heard the following statement many times: "I don't know what I would do if I couldn't _____ (you fill in the blank)." This statement captures the problem. People seem to think changing a habit is a process of deprivation. We see changing a habit as if we are losing something that makes us happy. Well, that is probably the way habits ultimately serve us over a long period of time. We think we need them to remain happy and comfortable. The procrastination habit is no different.

I believe procrastination can be eliminated from anyone's life if a person just starts doing things that are the opposite of procrastination. There are certain things you can start doing that will just choke out procrastination. If you can develop the habit of doing these things, procrastination doesn't have a chance. You can compare eliminating procrastination to getting rid of weeds in your lawn. If you have a lawn full of weeds, you don't go out and try to individually pull every weed. What you want to do is stimulate growth of your grass, and if you can do that, the weeds will eventually be choked out—permanently! There won't be room for the weeds to grow because the root structure of your grass will be too strong. Your yard will be in the "habit" of growing grass instead of weeds.

In this analogy of growing grass, let me point out that the key to success is on how you strategically view the weed issue. If you focus on how to get rid of the weeds, that's where you will spend your time, money, and energy. If, however, you focus on how to make your grass grow, that is how you will invest your effort. To overcome procrastination, the same attitude will work: Don't focus on how you can stop procrastinating. Instead, focus on what you can do to get more accomplished. If you focus on doing things that will move the results needle, your procrastination habit will eventually be choked out. There won't be room for it to be active.

If you practice PBP, you will begin to develop habits that will choke out procrastination. *Remember, PBP means that you start doing things immediately, regardless of what you think you need to make it perfect.* It may mean that you will have to rework some details, but you will still get things done faster. If you don't think you have all the information you need, start anyway! If you don't have all the tools you need, start anyway! If you do something that turns out to be wrong, use the mistake to make your next effort better.

❝*Better to do something imperfectly than to do nothing flawlessly.*❞
—Robert H. Schuller

Practicing the concept of PBP has revolutionized my life and my business. The basic premise is that procrastination is thrown out the window by simply taking action *now*. Even if I can't do it perfectly today, it's all right. Obviously, brain surgery is exempt from this idea, but in lots of cases, the acceptable level of quality is not as significant as the results achieved by getting the job done *now*.

I regularly communicate with my customers to see why they like to do business with me. I want to know if I am maintaining my competitive position in their eyes and what I can do better and faster to help them become more effective. I consistently hear my customers say they give me contracts and projects because they know the work will be done quickly, with deadlines always met, if not finished ahead of schedule.

I will admit that my team's work environment can be quite hectic when we have a critical job to do with little time to do it, but my team understands the importance of speed, and we're willing to do whatever it takes to meet deadlines and exceed customer expectations. Speedy completion of work gives us the opportunity to do more work—and more work means higher revenues, greater productivity, and more profits. Because our compensation plans reward productivity and speed, this translates into more money for everyone.

Go as Far as You Can See, and Then You'll See Farther

The principle of going as far as you can see and then being able to see farther is the basic justification for practicing PBP. It is also a concept that has the power to nip procrastination in the bud before it has a chance to flower. The basic justification for procrastination is the *alleged* need to wait until you can see more. If you begin to take action based on going as far as you can see, it will begin to choke procrastination because you can always see something! You don't have to understand all the details between where you are and where you want to be. Remember, the *Apollo* moon mission was off course 90 percent of the time, but NASA was able to make continual course corrections and land at the correct spot. If NASA engineers had waited until they possessed the technology to keep the craft on course 100 percent of the time before they were willing to launch the mission, we may never have achieved a successful moon landing.

> **❝If I'd had some set idea of a finish line, don't you think I would have crossed it years ago?❞**
> —Bill Gates

Several of my best customers are major corporations serving the direct marketing industry. These companies provide significant career opportunities for individuals who have a desire to start their own business and become extremely successful. Among the associates within all of these organizations, there is a wide range of success. These companies spend a lot of money, time, and effort trying to help their associates maximize their effectiveness and become highly successful. The associates in these companies who have the greatest degree of success fully embrace the principle of going as far as they can see, so they can see farther. Building any direct marketing business is a process in which certain basic things must be accomplished:

- A base of customers must be built.
- A network of associates must be created.
- Product expertise and knowledge must be acquired.
- Basic sales skills must be learned.

Those who fail in direct marketing efforts usually fail to put together the basic pieces that will ensure their success. They try to travel farther and faster than they can legitimately see, and they lose sight of what they should be doing today.

A logical question to ask is "How do I determine how far I can see?" The answer to this question is found in the process I outlined concerning focus, in Chapters 4 and 5. You recall that a major piece of that process was to factually determine current conditions, which is done by identifying strategic negatives and strategic positives. Identifying those factors exposes a number of things: opportunities, shortcomings, and high-leverage activities on which to focus. Focusing on those high-leverage activities is the starting point for going as far as you can see, and the key to success.

Appendix C will guide you through creating your Execution Blueprint, which will give you further insight on what you need to do to maximize your present efforts and to make sure you don't get too far ahead of yourself. As part of the Execution Blueprint, you will complete a More Of/Less Of (MOLO) Matrix (Exercise 16 in Appendix C), which identifies the things you do that produce the greatest impact, as well as what may actually be reducing your overall effectiveness.

The MOLO Matrix will help you move the results needle by showing you:

1. What is working well and what is not as you pursue your vision
2. What you need to change to be more effective
3. The high-leverage activities that deserve the majority of your time and effort

As part of this exercise, you will be led through four questions, described in the following sections.

1. What do you need to do more of?

This question helps you identify what you need to continue doing to increase your results.

Ava is a sales manager who is charged with the task of prioritizing the efforts of her sales team. She determined that her salespeople needed to spend more time making cold calls to prospective customers. Her team members, however, had not been doing much of this, and their experience level was marginal in making these types of calls. When her salespeople began to make these calls on a regular basis, they began to build experience on what works and what doesn't. They are also practicing PBP because they are doing things before they can do them perfectly—but they are at least doing something by making calls!

Marginal experience can also be described as not being able to see very far with respect to the outcomes. This experience enabled Ava's team to see farther. Since pushing her team to make more cold calls, they have closed an average of 37 percent more business in the past three months, with ever-increasing weekly averages.

2. What do you need to do less of?

Here you will identify what you do that wastes time or is not effective.

In my book *We've Got to Stop Meeting Like This* (available in the bookstore at www.tonyjeary.com), I talk about how ineffective meetings suck away operational time and greatly contribute to a lack of results. I have a client who used to be especially weak in this area. Not only did he conduct inefficient meetings, but he also conducted a *lot* of them, which had a direct and negative impact on his team's productivity. Moreover, his employees' morale was being affected: A corporate survey indicated high levels of frustration with demands on their time and his employees' low respect for management. My client finally realized that he needed to have fewer meetings in general and that the meetings he did have needed to be better executed.

Before he began to work with me to become more organizationally efficient, he was guilty of not preparing, having impromptu meetings with no regard for other time constraints, not creating and following an agenda, never starting or ending on time, and feeling that nothing really happened after these meetings, beyond attending more meetings. I helped him work through some operating standards that he now applies to his own meeting routine and that he insists his team follow as well. Some of his standards include:

- When planning a meeting, include a detailed agenda in the meeting request.

- Start and end on time, no matter what.
- Designate a scribe or note-taker to capture action items for follow-up, a summary of which must be sent immediately after the meeting.
- Create a "parking lot" to table side items that arise but are not on the agenda.
- Prepare in advance all necessary materials and send to the team before the meeting.

My client has created a culture of better meeting efficiency by doing less of the things that were really taking away from his time—and his team's. They are now better able to focus on their primary goals and objectives. A recent corporate survey indicates that team members feel that their time is being better spent and that they are generally less frustrated.

3. What do you need to start doing?

This question asks you to think of things you are not doing that could be important to getting better results.

Personally, I know that delegating effectively has a tremendous impact on my results. I have a team of highly talented individuals who support my vision, and I continually ask them to handle things on my behalf. Some of the approaches I take toward my delegation include:

- Asking my staff to handle actions (including correspondence, filing, mailings, running errands) that otherwise consume time I could spend more effectively as a leader
- Making daily lists that detail actions and priorities
- Having daily follow-up meetings to check status and to break through bottlenecks
- Noting e-mail subject lines with "action required" or "response requested"

- Contracting with outside partners or consultants when we are stretched for time or expertise internally

I estimate that the above tasks provide me with at least two "extra" hours a day that I can better spend talking with prospective clients and building the business. I have created a culture wherein my team members are always thinking of how to spend their time most effectively while communicating honestly and frequently about progress and problems. As a result, we are efficient and streamlined, able to exceed our customers' expectations, and see real success—as evidenced by our bottom line. Each year, I see an increase in my company's revenue and a decrease in inefficiencies that distract from growth.

4. What do you need to stop doing?

Here you'll identify low-impact, time-wasting activities to eliminate from your daily habits. These activities could be minor, such as spending too much time on the telephone with colleagues, helping others out on nonemergency items while pushing aside your more critical tasks, inefficiently preparing for meetings, and generally allowing small things to push you away from your primary objectives.

These activities could also be *major*. Instead of delegating to your staff, perhaps you're spending several hours a day on tasks that would be better handled by others, which reduces your ability to meet critical deadlines. For example, instead of returning phone calls to the company's insurance provider, ask someone in HR to manage it. Don't conduct basic research; ask your assistant to do it instead.

Maybe your fondness for micromanagement is causing resentment in your colleagues and delaying progress because your continual henpecking for status updates results in high turnover. I used to work with a fellow who constantly barraged his team with requests for status updates. Every day he sent endless e-mails to the team, detailing what they had accomplished, what needed to be done, why it hadn't been done, and what was going to happen next. Although a culture of communication and status updates can really help with productivity, *too many* requests can ruin morale and suck away valuable time. After repeated complaints from his team, he now limits his status checks to once a day and most of the time does not even need to request them. He has created voluntary change by easing up on his staff, who more readily communicate with him instead of resenting the frequent intrusions.

Perhaps there are some hard organizational changes that need to be made from staffing or responsibility perspectives, changes that would improve overall production. In the past I've had the unfortunate task of letting employees go. In management, this is just a fact of life, but it never gets easier. I once had an employee who was a terrific person but just not efficient enough for the fast pace of my organization. Her agonizing attention to meaningless details slowed everyone's productivity. Additionally, she wasn't as organized or neat as I needed her to be, and in her absence (which was frequent) we could not quickly find important documents or follow-up items. Luckily, I had a friend who operated a small company and needed a part-time assistant. He hired this employee, and the match turned out to be a good one for them. In return, I was able to hire someone who better suited my organization's hectic demands. Making this change freed up emotional worry on my part and enabled the rest of my team to regain the clockwork efficiency that really defines what we offer our clients.

There are real impediments to your productivity, and they need to be exposed. Beyond honestly identifying them, however, you must make the commitment to eliminate them from your daily routine. This may sound easy, but habits are hard to change! It will take real devotion from you, so when you start to buckle, think about your vision, why you want it, and how *wasting time is just going to push you farther away from where you want to go.* Once you eliminate these time wasters, you'll have greater focus and be able to better tackle the high-leverage actions that feed your success.

Summary

Procrastination is a bad habit that greatly restricts results and effectiveness, but it can be controlled. The first step is to identify the reasons behind it, then make the commitment to move toward production, the opposite of procrastination. Production is the completion of tasks and projects in reduced time frames, and it is greatly accelerated by the concept of Production Before Perfection (PBP). Rather than waiting for every aspect of a project to come into perfect, linear alignment, PBP allows you to manage the aspects in parallel, adjust the project as you progress, and reach greater results.

The concept of PBP will be uncomfortable for others at first, however, so you will need to be persuasive and persistent to effect voluntary change. The next chapter will help you alter others' attitudes and behavior through images of influence, an understanding of which will boost your persuasion power and increase your communication effectiveness.

Very Important Points

▶ Of the things you can actually control about your production, one habit has more impact on delaying results than any other: *procrastination*. We all are guilty of procrastination to some extent. There are two kinds:

1. Positive procrastination: This is when you legitimately need some "mental percolation" time to gather your thoughts and get clear on what you need to do.
2. Negative procrastination: This is based on some pretty flimsy excuses to avoid doing something, which will ultimately affect your results in negative ways.

▶ The principle of going as far as you can see and then being able to see farther is the basic justification for practicing Production Before Perfection (PBP).

▶ PBP means that you start doing things immediately, regardless of what you think you need to make them perfect. Rather than waiting for every aspect of a project to come into perfect, linear alignment, PBP allows you to manage the aspects in parallel, adjust the project as you progress, and reach greater results.

CHAPTER 8

The Persuasive Influence of Strategic Presence

☞ *Your ability to persuade others requires an authentic persona that is based on your own values and behavior.*

Chapter 7 discussed the second leg of the execution tripod: production, which is the ability to complete actions in reduced time frames. Production can be sped up by using the Production Before Perfection (PBP) concept of starting work at the outset and working in parallel progress, instead of waiting for every aspect to line up.

This chapter details presence, the third leg in the tripod. Presence is important as you go about pursuing your vision because you will need to enlist the help of others to help you take action on your behalf. To be most persuasive and create voluntary change, you must understand how others perceive you, which will help you communicate more effectively.

I have a friend who is an elementary school teacher who shared the following story with me. In the middle of the school year, a new pupil who had come from another country was enrolled. The student was uncomfortable in the new environment, and the other kids in the class were doing what kids do: there was a lot of giggling and staring and posturing for the new arrival. The new student was dressed in a way that did not meet the expectations of a few of the other children, and eventually one of them (the class clown) began to make jokes about the new student's appearance. The new student was embarrassed and tried to ignore the harassment. Soon a couple of other kids in the class joined in the childish attack.

As the scene was on the verge of chaos and the teacher was about to intervene, a girl in the class stood up and told everyone to stop picking on their new classmate. She reminded them that it was scary to be new in a school and they needed to be kind to the student and make her feel welcome. She reminded them that they should treat this new person as they would want to be treated if they were in a new country and a new school. The class had a lot of respect for this girl, and the scene quickly settled down.

After class, the teacher thanked the girl who had quieted the situation and said, "That was a very brave thing you did. Why did you do that?" She said, "Because that is what my mom and dad would expect me to do."

I love this story because it so powerfully illustrates the power and effect of what I call *strategic presence*. The girl had merely done what she knew her parents would want her to do. Her perception and understanding of her parents' values persuaded her to defend the new student. The parents of that courageous little girl had succeeded in creating a positive strategic presence in her mind, which gave her the willingness and courage to do what she did. Most important, the parents' strategic presence was so authentic that they did not have to be physically present to inspire their daughter's good behavior. Her parents' values had become values she also embraced. Those values persuaded and empowered her to do what she did, voluntarily.

Your "Strategic Presence" Defines Other People's Perception of You

An impression of you exists in the mind of every person with whom you have a personal or professional relationship. It is a persona-identifying presence that defines the total perception others have about you. It is this overall persona I am referring to when I use the term strategic presence. You constantly create two types of strategic presence: *positive* strategic presence and *negative* strategic presence. I'll say more about the characteristics of positive and negative presence later, but for now I ask just that you understand that both types of strategic presence are realities and you are always creating both. You know this is true because you have no trouble ticking off a list of the positive and negative qualities of everyone you know. It's just that some people have more positive attributes that reflect their strategic presence than negative attributes, and vice versa.

Before I get into how strategic presence is created and transmitted, I want to talk about the real effect your strategic presence has on others' attitudes and behaviors, and why. The most important fact about strategic presence is that it produces two possible reactions in others. It either produces *voluntary cooperation* or it produces various forms of *resistance*. If the people in your communication universe have lots of positive impressions about your strategic presence, they will be more likely to support what you want, most of the time.

If, on the other hand, most of their perceptions of your strategic presence are negative, they will be unlikely to support what you want, and they may even actively try to undermine your efforts. Their resistance can be active or passive, but they won't be persuaded to voluntarily exceed expectations.

So the possibilities concerning how your strategic presence impacts others are limited to cooperation or resistance, and there is not much middle ground between them. As someone once said, "You are either for us or against us." Because these are the two alternatives, it is easy to see why creating an authentic, positive strategic presence is critical in the execution of your vision (your goals, targets, requests, etc.).

❝*Creating an authentic, positive strategic presence is critical in the execution of your vision.*❞

I want to be very clear when I say that creating a positive strategic presence is not intended to be a strategy of manipulation. The positive strategic presence you project must be real, and it must be perceived as authentic. Failing the test of authenticity means the very image you hope to establish will be perceived as deceptive and disingenuous, or worse. Your positive, authentic strategic presence has to present who you really are, and it can't be faked. People are very perceptive, and they will detect efforts to project a phony persona for the purposes of manipulating behavior.

So you may ask, "Why don't I just let my strategic presence be what it is, and not be concerned about it?" That is a great question. The answer is simple.

You create strategic presence regardless of how aware you are of the process. Some people just let it happen, and lots of erroneous perceptions are developed about their persona along the way because they were not aware of what was happening to them. Their lack of awareness about creating strategic presence meant they were not proactive in the process. Have you ever heard anyone complain about being "misunderstood" and seen their amazement to discover what people thought about them, their motives, and what they were really about? Well, that is a risk of what can happen when you don't take a proactive stance in the process of creating your strategic presence.

Fortunately, there are specific things you can do to protect yourself against false perceptions taking root. Once false perceptions take root, they will produce resistance, and it is extremely difficult to root out false perceptions. As you know, perception is reality, and once people have something firmly entrenched in their belief window, it is hard to remove it. If you allow false perceptions to take root in the minds of others, you may be perceived as deceptive, and people will second-guess and resist you at every turn.

The Building Blocks of Strategic Presence

Now I want to discuss how strategic presence is created. What about you speaks the loudest about who you are? What is it about you that is most likely to create the perceptions others will develop about who you are? What are the components and the building blocks of those perceptions? Essentially, two components contribute to your strategic presence: your values and your behavior.

Your Values Contribute to Your Strategic Presence

To discover your values, you need to look no further than your own belief window. Your values are established by what you believe to be right, wrong, true, false, acceptable, unacceptable, appropriate, and inappropriate. Let's face it, as you have lived your life, you have developed deep, strong opinions about many things. Your opinions spring forth from your values, and your values play a huge role in influencing what you do.

❝*Trust always affects two measurable outcomes—speed and cost. When trust goes down, speed goes down and cost goes up. This creates a trust tax. When trust goes up, speed goes up and cost goes down. This creates a trust dividend. It's that simple, that predictable.***❞**
—Stephen M. R. Covey

Unfortunately, your own perceptions or opinions about your values may or may not line up with your real values. People are very capable of believing they have specific values about certain things, but their own behavior contradicts what they say. It's the "what you do is so loud, I can't hear what you say" scenario in action. So testing and really identifying your own values may not be as simple as it seems. In other words, just because you say you have certain values does not mean you practice them! It is only as you practice your values on a daily basis, through good times and bad, that they project authenticity and weight.

Identifying values and measuring them is rather like goal setting, in that much has been written on the subject. There are many excellent guides and methods you can use to help identify your values (for example, my *Designing Your Own Life* binder, available in the bookstore at www.tonyjeary.com, helps you determine what you really want out of life and how to set goals to achieve it). The point I want to make is that this is a worthwhile exercise. You just need to select a method and do it, because for the purposes of creating strategic presence, you need an understanding of your values.

The list of every value you have can be very long, to the extent that you may have trouble dealing with all of them. My approach to values is that they shape what you actually do, and what you do creates strategic presence. So, if only for that reason, being aware of your values and being able to state them is important. Obviously, you do many things, and some of the things you do are more important than others. It is the values you have that dominate the things you do that are relevant to the creation of strategic presence. That leads to the discussion of the second building block of strategic presence, which is your behavior.

Your Behavior Also Contributes to Your Strategic Presence

With respect to persuading others to exceed expectations, there are five categories of action (in other words, the things you do) that have a significant influence on creating strategic presence:

1. Work ethic
2. Integrity
3. Judgment
4. Courage
5. Willingness to help others

Let's take a look at each of these actions in more detail.

1. Your work ethic: Regardless of where you work (from your home, in an office, in a restaurant, driving a cab, with the public, in a factory, or anywhere else), you will still occasionally seek the assistance and support of others and specifically want them to become willing to exceed expectations. Therefore, the work ethic issue is very significant. If your strategic presence does not illuminate your own work ethic in a way that demonstrates you are willing to do what you ask others to do, your positive strategic presence in this area will be damaged. Your personal work ethic is represented by the many things you do, but the most visible elements of your work ethic are the things you do that impact the time and effort of others.

> **"Being aware of your values and being able to state them is important."**

Moreover, the things you do that impact others are relatively simple things, like being on time and keeping appointments. When you are late for meetings, phone calls, and project deadlines, it creates a poor perception of your work ethic. Your perceived work ethic is also impacted by how you are perceived as an initiator, rather than a responder. Do you proactively move forward on what needs to be done, or do you wait to be told to do it? People who initiate action are considered to be more participatory and opportunity oriented than passive responders.

2. Your integrity: Integrity is about keeping your word, communicating honestly, and doing what you say you will do, even if it hurts. People of integrity don't make decisions based on expediency. They make decisions based on doing the right thing. However, you must recognize that doing the right thing is easy when there is little at stake. The real test of integrity comes in times of temptation, stress, and pressure. It is in such times that people closely observe what you do, and your actions in those times become part of your strategic presence.

There is a saying that "when you are jostled, the content of your character spills out." It is the part of you that spills out when jostled that exposes your integrity. People of integrity also admit their mistakes and follow through on their commitments. It may seem trite to say that for people of integrity, their word is their bond, but that is the core issue of integrity.

3. Your judgment: If you are in a leadership position, the welfare, safety, and general well-being of those under your care is directly impacted by your judgment under fire. When your judgment fails to take the needs of others into consideration, it creates a negative perception and sends the message that you don't care about others. People will resist trusting and giving their emotional support to anyone who demonstrates poor judgment in their daily decision-making. Poor judgment creates a perception that the execution of your vision is probably not plausible or worthy of supporting because your judgment is suspect.

People who demonstrate good judgment are levelheaded and realistic. They are able to take in difficult information without flying off the handle and taking inappropriate action that is driven by fear. A person with good judgment handles pressure with grace and, most important, with confidence. This inspires others to handle pressure in the same way.

4. Your courage: Courage is demonstrated when others see how you handle adversity. My friend Zig Ziglar, the great motivational speaker, is a living example of this reality. Zig turned eighty-two in November 2008. On March 1, 2007, he experienced a fall during the night and suffered an injury that produced profound short-term memory loss. Overnight, this energetic man who has inspired millions of people for decades was no longer capable of speaking in the style he had presented for so many years. Zig Ziglar suddenly found himself in the middle of a lot of adversity. Lesser men would just quit and say "I've done enough."

Not so with Zig. He decided that being open and transparent about his injury and letting others know of his struggle would be a great inspiration for others going through times of adversity and trial. Zig has always taught others that it is not your circumstances that determine your success, it is what you do with your circumstances. He decided to make the most of his circumstances and demonstrate this powerful principle in his own life. Zig changed his onstage performances to an interview format that is facilitated by his editor, who is his youngest daughter, Julie. The title of both his presentation and his newest book is "Embrace the Struggle." Julie gently guides him through, around, and over points he tends to repeat because of his memory deficit, and she helps him stay on track with the information he wants to deliver. This is a great example of courage, and the strategic presence Zig Ziglar has achieved in the minds of his audiences is becoming even more powerful and authentic because of it.

5. Your willingness to help others: If you want others to help you, you must be willing to help them. Helping and appreciating others in this sense goes beyond just thanking them and sending them birthday cards, or being aware of their anniversary dates and children's names. Helping others involves understanding what they want in life, personally and professionally, and being willing to invest some of yourself in their goals.

Sometimes helping others might involve just encouraging them. Sometimes it might be just doing some little thing for them to be of assistance. Helping others does not have to involve a huge effort or expense, and you certainly can't be the solution to everyone's problems or take responsibility for their hope. However, your willingness to invest yourself in their lives and to exceed their expectations will become a significant building block of your own strategic presence in their minds.

I want to caution and remind you, however, that this is not intended to be a manipulative strategy. Nothing turns off people more than believing they are being helped so they will be obligated to return the favor.

How to Communicate Strategically

Transmitting the building blocks of strategic presence engages the way you communicate with others, and communication transcends mere words. Many people treat communication as a collection of skills, and they think of it as just another training or coaching objective. This type of thinking represents a *tactical* approach to communication. In contrast, I treat communication as a *strategic* issue that has great significance in facilitating the tripod of execution: persuasion, production, and presence. If you can visualize execution as a train rolling down a track to a predetermined destination, think of communication as the engine that pulls and powers the train. In that role, strategic communication has several specific objectives it must accomplish.

Remember, the building blocks of strategic presence are your values and your behavior. Strategic communication involves the actual transmission of those building blocks. The objective of strategic communication is to achieve a specific result with those you hope to persuade. You communicate strategically when you allow your messaging to be guided by

> **❝***The objective of strategic communication is to achieve a specific result with those you hope to persuade.***❞**

three tests, or standards. If your messaging does not meet one or more of these standards, your results will be diminished:

1. Your communication must impact others' beliefs.
2. You must communicate vision, strength, and opportunity.
3. You must communicate value.

Let's take a look at these three standards in more detail.

Standard #1: Your Communication Must Impact Others' Beliefs

Strategic communication involves transmitting points of view, and you must cast a vision for others they can accept, embrace, and consider worthy of supporting enthusiastically. This requires communication that will impact people at the level of belief. Communication that is not perceived to be authentic will not be effective in achieving this objective, because messages that are not authentic will not be believed. Three components contribute to message authenticity:

1. The first component of authenticity is to tell the truth. If anyone in your communication universe perceives he or she is not being told the truth, you will lose that person immediately.
2. The second component of authenticity is commitment. If people do not believe you are as committed as you

expect them to be, you will lose them. You must demonstrate your commitment by what you do.

3. The third component of authenticity is motive. People want to know why you are asking them to support you, and this involves how well they understand your motives. What do you hope to get out of what you're asking, and what do you want them to get out of it? Communicating your motives requires sharing your heart with others.

Standard #2: You Must Communicate Vision, Strength, and Opportunity

Whenever you communicate, it is wise to touch on these next three items and relate your message to them. People need to be exposed regularly to these important concepts so they may strengthen their perception about the value and importance of their effort:

1. **Communicate your vision:** Your vision has the power to pull you and others across the gap from current conditions to your goal. To do that, you must ensure that your vision is kept in the forefront of people's awareness. Whenever you construct messages to those you hope to inspire, that is an opportunity to attach relevance of what you are trying to accomplish to your vision.

2. **Communicate strength:** Inspiring confidence in others is critical to success. Confidence involves people being convinced they have the ability to do what is being asked of them. If there is doubt—yours or theirs— about their ability to be successful, that doubt will diminish the results. For this reason, you must consistently talk about the collective and individual strengths they have that will support success. Nothing instills

confidence in people more than understanding the capability they have to be successful, and much of that comes when they really understand their strengths.

3. **Communicate the opportunity:** To create enthusiasm and promote voluntary change, leaders must constantly remind people of the opportunities that exist for them if they successfully execute the correct strategies and objectives. Everyone is interested in "What's in it for me?" and you can best communicate that by articulating the opportunities that will flow out of success.

Whenever you communicate about any initiative, project, or task, you should relate the desired effort to these three points. Essentially, ask yourself the following questions to make sure you're on track in communicating vision, strength, and opportunity:

1. How does what we are about to do help move us closer to our vision?
2. What strengths do we have that provide the ability and the expertise to be successful?
3. What new opportunities can we expect if we are successful?

Standard #3: You Must Communicate Value

Here, I'm not talking about communicating your *personal* values. Instead, I'm talking about communicating the *real* value of your vision and your enterprise.

Some things never change, and the need to communicate value is one of those things. Strategic communication always frames itself in relationship to value and value creation. Communicating value goes beyond merely stating what you do and how you do it. You successfully articulate value when you speak to the strategic benefit your vision, strategies, and objectives have for others.

You are best able to articulate relevant value to others when you understand their felt needs. Communicating value connects powerfully with felt need, and when you connect with felt need, people are able to be inspired and cooperative. So addressing others' felt needs and relating the value of your effort to meeting those needs will have a strategic effect on what people are willing to do. It will also play a significant role in transmitting your strategic presence.

When you communicate using these standards as a measuring stick for your messaging, you are communicating strategically and transmitting your strategic presence proactively and effectively. After all, your messages reflect your values and your behavior, which are the two building blocks of strategic presence.

Creating Images of Influence

Communication that produces strategic presence also involves creating what I call *images of influence*. The images of influence you create affect others' perceptions, attitudes, and behavior in a subtle but powerful way. The authenticity of these images of influence is vitally important to your success. In fact, the perceived authenticity of your strategic presence may very well pivot on the images of influence you create and deploy.

As you have learned, Strategic Acceleration incorporates the need and ability to persuade others to consistently exceed expectations. This level of performance requires voluntary change, and it requires changes in the belief windows of the people you are attempting to persuade. Belief windows are changed only through new personal experiences and new information that is accepted as truth. Because more than 90 percent of communication is nonverbal, much of the new information people accept as truth is based on their perceptions. Images of influence provide the fuel for many of those perceptions and are a primary factor in your ability to motivate others to take action that will exceed expectations.

The images of influence you create are shaped by all the things others see about you. They are shaped in many ways—for example:

- Personally, images of influence could be shaped by how you treat your friends and loved ones, your grooming habits and wardrobe, and your reliability or punctuality.
- Professionally, images of influence could be shaped by the appearance of written materials, marketing and sales documents, and recruiting or training programs.

To create congruent and authentic images of influence for your strategic communication objectives, three strategic building blocks are important:

1. A vision statement
2. Behavioral priorities
3. Presence statements and characteristics

Let's look at each of these in a bit more detail.

Your Vision Statement

A vision statement expresses your hope and the great goal you have for the future. A vision statement is a specific statement that articulates the future as fact and gives others clarity about your vision. As you go about creating your vision statement, you should consider what you want, why you want it, and what positive things will happen when your vision is executed.

For example, I have a client who has the following vision statement:

> My vision is to be a strong, strategic asset to my company by continually focusing on long-term benefits for the organization; making decisions based on creating job and financial security for its people; and furthering my legacy to "just do your job, and do it well," which will subsequently create more of the same results I seek.

Exercise 17 in Appendix C will help you create a vision statement of your own.

Your Behavioral Priorities

These priorities address the behaviors you most value and expect in yourself and others. When people understand what is most important to you, they understand your priorities and what matters most to you concerning their own behavior.

For example, if two of your most valued behaviors involve knowing how to ask good questions and being an active listener, you need to communicate the importance of those behaviors by teaching and training those skills. You must also demonstrate those same skills in your own everyday activities. Exercise 18 in Appendix C will guide you through identifying your own behaviors, which will become images of influence that people will carry with them as your strategic presence.

Presence Statements and Characteristics

It is important to understand what you are and what you want to be. It's equally important to know what you're *not* and what you do not want to be. Exercise 19 in Appendix C will help you identify your own characteristics, which need to be something you teach, talk about, and reflect in all you say and do. They become statements that form images of influence that transmit strategic presence.

Personal examples might be:

I am:

- *Disciplined and hardworking*
- *Empathetic and sensitive to others' needs*
- *Deadline-driven and team-oriented*

I do not:

- *Procrastinate and give others the bulk of the burden*
- *Pursue my agenda and goals without concern for others*
- *Show up late or miss deadlines*

Work examples might be:

We are:

- *Proactive and engaging problem solvers*
- *Responsible for our successes and failures*
- *Responsive to our customers' needs*

We do not:

- *Restrict the creativity of others*
- *Gossip or perpetuate false rumors*
- *Procrastinate or delay action*

Why These Building Blocks Are Important

The three building blocks above establish the strategic "what" on which images of influence are based. When you create your own presence statements, they become rudders and training wheels for your behavior, which creates strategic presence.

Creating and Sustaining a Positive Strategic Presence Requires Repetition

All strategic communication requires repetition. Just telling someone something a couple of times does not guarantee he or she will "get it." In that respect, creating and sustaining positive strategic presence is the result of a constant drip of messaging and activity that strengthens, affirms, and solidifies perceptions. You must be sure that the positive messaging you want to communicate that relates to establishing your strategic presence is ongoing.

I want to be clear about this: *Never* think you can say too much about the strategic issues that contribute to your strategic presence and that influence voluntary change in others. It is a sad reality that we live in an age where your positive strategic presence can become a negative perception very quickly.

An extreme example of this reality involves the late Ken Lay, former CEO of the now disgraced Enron, which collapsed in scandal. Prior to Enron's demise, Lay was a positive role model and a most respected corporate leader. Enron was viewed as one of the most progressive and successful examples of creative business strategies for the twenty-first century. The positive strategic presence Lay enjoyed was embraced by everyone he touched.

Suddenly, when his company failed, Lay became the pariah of American business. Lay and his associates were attacked and vilified by elected officials and the same peers who used to laud his leadership. All of this change was the result of an almost instantaneous flip in his strategic presence from highly positive to highly negative.

I believe that if Lay had practiced and deployed all the principles I've discussed regarding strategic presence, the Enron scandal would have never happened. That may sound like an arrogant statement, but think about it. Enron was not clear about its values, and it resulted in some very bad behavior. The company's senior managers made decisions based on expediency and not on what was right. They failed the courage test and every other point I've made in this chapter. They did not build their enterprise on vision, strength, and opportunity. Instead, they built it on short-term survival needs and personal greed. The strategic presence of the Enron leadership group was not authentic, and it came crashing down upon their heads.

Do you see that strategic presence is a serious matter? In creating it, you are continually reminded to pursue your vision based on principles of significance that last and that require you to constantly evaluate and measure your own values and behavior—i.e., the two building blocks of strategic presence. If Lay had put Enron's business activities through the filters that create strategic presence, all of the company's criminal and public disgrace may have been avoided. Enron's senior managers might have had to make some hard decisions about how to solve their business problems, but they would not have been perceived as the personification of corporate evil.

Summary

Of the three legs of the execution tripod, strategic presence is the most subjective. Strategic presence dwells in the land of perception, and it is hard to manage and control perception. A positive strategic presence presents characteristics that build credibility, trust, and a spirit of cooperation. In contrast, a negative strategic presence sows seeds of suspicion, distrust, and rebellion. You have the ability to proactively create a positive strategic presence by communicating strategically and building images of influence that reflect your values and behavior. A strong strategic presence positively affects execution and results.

Very Important Points

▶ An impression of you exists in the mind of every person with whom you have a personal or professional relationship. It is a persona-identifying presence that defines the total perception others have about you.

▶ Two strategic issues are most responsible for creating the persona that establishes your strategic presence in the minds of others: your values and your behavior.

▶ The images of influence you create affect others' perceptions, attitudes, and behavior in a subtle but powerful way. The authenticity of these images of influence is vitally important to your success.

CONCLUSION

I n the introduction to *Strategic Acceleration,* I made several promises to you that I hope I have kept. I promised to tell you about strategic concepts that would transform the way you think, live, and work. I promised that you would forever change the way you think of results, and this would help you become more effective. And I promised you *clarity* about what you really want, the ability to *focus* on high-leverage activities, and *execution* strategies that will really move the results needle. Reading and putting this book's suggestions into practice fall into three categories of skill—good, great, and mastery:

- You are operating on the *good* level if you do what is necessary to achieve clarity about what you want.
- When operating on the *great* level, you will do what is necessary to achieve clarity and learn to focus on the high-leverage activities that have the greatest impact on your results.
- But you will see the most success when you operate on the *mastery* level. When you gain real clarity, get focused, and execute your vision using the principles of persuasion, production, and presence, you will produce excellence and exceed expectations.

I know there is a lot of information in this book, and processing it all could feel a bit overwhelming at first. You might be wondering, "What are the most important elements of

Strategic Acceleration? If I did only one of the things suggested in this book, what would it be? What one thing in Strategic Acceleration would most likely improve my results and move me to the mastery level even if I ignore everything else?"

> **"A good objective of leadership is to help those who are doing poorly to do well and to help those who are doing well to do even better."**
> —Jim Rohn

My answer is this: Strategic Acceleration is a *complete* way of thinking, and *each* of its pieces is equally important. You can't understand what you really want without clarity. Without knowing what you want, focus is diminished. Without clarity and focus, execution becomes suspect. Strategic Acceleration really is a tripod, and each of its three legs is necessary to keep the tripod upright and functional. So please don't shortcut the details that pertain to each leg of the tripod, or you will not get the full benefit of this book.

As I explained in Chapter 7, Production Before Perfection, having a place to begin is more important than worrying about all of the details before you move forward. When you're overwhelmed with tasks and feel unsure about what to do, the best tactic is often simply to *begin;* otherwise, procrastination and inactivity set in. Now that you've read this book and are primed to make valuable changes for the better and start down your own personal Strategic Acceleration path, you just need to know where to begin. I recommend getting more clear on what you really want.

If you do not know what you really want, you forever will be pursuing vague ideas that have little chance of becoming reality. I've spent many years working with a lot of intelligent, successful people. These people make things happen at a high level, yet all of them have been able to enhance their effectiveness by improving their clarity about what they really want.

I wish I had videos to show the facial expressions people make when they really get clear about what they want. Their eyes get big, and they begin to get excited about pursuing their vision. Suddenly there is light where there was murkiness. They see solutions rather than problems. Their path to achievement becomes firm, and they know where to put their feet. Clarity alone produces all these things.

I believe most people really want to do well in life. I don't think people begin their lives planning to live in insignificance. Instead, most people want to make a difference. They want to be respected and valued. They want to feel their lives have meaning, substance, and importance. Far too many people never achieve these feelings of satisfaction because they experience early failures in their lives and they never figure out that it does not have to be a way of life. When someone experiences repeated failures, it is easy for that person to become discouraged and give up on his or her dreams and hopes of significance. When someone is in that condition, it is very difficult for him to revitalize himself, regain the optimism of youth, and try again. But clarity is the principle that can reignite that spark of hope. A clear vision pulls you toward focus and execution.

The epiphany I see in the eyes of people who come to my Strategic Acceleration Studio when they get clear on what they want is actually the first glimmer of this pulling effect. Call it the "Albert Mensah effect" if you like: In Chapter 2, I described how Albert saw an American movie with people wearing shoes, and he got clarity about what he really wanted, and even a herd of undisciplined equines would not have been able to stop him from getting to America! Albert knew nothing about the technical aspects of focus and the importance of persuasion, production, and strategic presence. Albert just got clear on what he wanted, and that was all he needed to start to pursue his dream. Clarity was enough of a starting point, and from there he developed focus and ultimately was able to execute his dream.

- After you are clear on your vision, which is simply knowing what you want to do and why you want to do it, the next challenge will be to focus on it. The success of your vision pivots on having the ability to identify and concentrate on the actions that will accelerate its progress, and filter out the distractions that will hinder it.

- Regardless of your current level of focus, you could probably improve your skills, and realizing that fact is the first step up the Effectiveness Ladder described in Chapter 4. From there, you'll be able to clarify the need to better focus, and thereby make a choice to spend time and energy on improvement activities. After that, it's all practice! Focus is a skill that can be learned and improved, and just like any other skill, the more conscious time you spend on its improvement, the more positive results and success you'll see. At the same time, you'll be unconsciously training your mind to consider these skills as second nature, or something you do without even really thinking about it, which is another way to describe a habit. And what a great habit to ingrain in your mind! I have seen individuals and groups transcend their own mind-sets about their ability to focus and go from scattered and distracted to pinpointed and organized, just by using sheer will based on a desire to improve.

- I know that once you see the real benefits that occur when you can filter out the noise and drive toward completing high-leverage activities, you'll be hooked on this new way of thinking. You'll have fewer distractions because you'll know them when they creep up, and you'll be able to squelch their effects before they take hold. You will consistently meet (and possibly even exceed) deadlines, which will free up attention and reduce worry—and delight those around you. You'll spend less time chasing down unimportant details and picking up where you left off before you became distracted, which will free up time to spend in any way you choose, whether for professional gain or personal enjoyment.

- All you need to do is take an honest look at where you are right now, compared to where you really want to be. Between the two points lie the high-leverage activities on which you need to focus to shift your location and close the gap. You'll know exactly what you need to do and how you need to spend your time to realize your vision, which, of course, will set you up for consistent execution.

- Clarity and focus provide your plan of "what" and "how," but when it's time to get things done, it's all about actually doing it. This might sound simple, maybe even overly so, but this is where you're going to spend most of your time. Approaching it well-prepared and with the right philosophy will make all the difference toward your success. I hope you remember the three P's of the execution tripod: persuasion, production, and presence.

- Using strong persuasion skills, you'll be able to get support from others who can help you execute and will undoubtedly benefit from your success. Being able to clearly and confidently state why your vision is authentic and important is the key to persuasion. From there, you'll be well-aligned for production, or getting things done faster and more efficiently.

- This requires you to practice Production Before Perfection (PBP), which is a terrific way to combat procrastination, because you get started and continue to work in parallel progress instead of waiting for every single detail to come into perfect harmony. Before you know it, you'll actually be finished with a task or project, while others without the PBP mind-set are still fooling around and banking on tomorrow. This will enable you to really stretch your paradigms and see where you can *really* go, which will undoubtedly be far beyond what you thought you were capable of reaching.

- But for ultimate execution, you need to do more than just convince people to support you and help you knock out stuff on your to-do list. Using your *strategic presence*, you need to engender voluntary change, which is long-lasting and will have far-reaching effects. Your positive actions and behaviors will inspire others to exceed expectations consistently and wholeheartedly, with courage, good judgment, and integrity.

I sincerely hope this book has exceeded *your* expectations. The information has grown from my desire to help you accelerate the positive results of your personal and professional life. I wanted to give you a practical methodology to move forward with confidence every day and pursue the boundless opportunities that exist for you when you get clear on what you really want, focus on what is necessary to achieve that vision, and execute with power. The following appendices contain exercises that will walk you through the thought-changing processes you must embrace to succeed at the speed of life. I wish you tremendous success!

APPENDIX A

Creating Your Clarity Blueprint

☞ *Acquiring clarity and increasing effectiveness will accelerate your success.*

Just as constructing a building requires a detailed plan, so does reconstructing how you approach your success. You need to know *what* you want to do, *why* you want to do it, and *how* you will do it. You also need to know the *benefit* of doing it, and the *negative payoff* for not doing it. This appendix will help you think through and document everything you'll need to effect positive change, either personal or organizational. It also becomes the baseline that helps you keep everything together as you execute your plans, and it will enable you to measure your success, through frequent review.

Creating a Clarity Blueprint

A *Clarity Blueprint* is really just a very detailed description of your personal Clarity Equation:

$$\frac{\text{what} + \text{why}}{\text{purpose} + \text{value}} = \text{clarity}$$

To better help you understand the principles behind Strategic Acceleration while building your Clarity Blueprint (templates for which can be downloaded at www.tonyjeary. com), you'll be guided through the following exercises:

Exercise 1: Create Voluntary Change: Create a change audit to see how to better spend your time.

Exercise 2: Understand Your Influences: Describe your belief window, or how you see the world and make all decisions.

Exercise 3: Understand Your Strategic Beliefs: Examine, then adjust how you think about your life.

Exercise 4: Outline What You Need to Do to Get What You Want: Create an action plan of small steps to reach your vision.

Exercise 5: Document Your Vision: Develop a clear vision to motivate yourself to change.

Exercise 6: Unlock Your Internal Keys to Success: Document your unique experiences, gifts, and talents that will help you succeed.

Exercise 7: Explore Where You Are Today, Why You Might Not Be Going Where You Want, and What Can Be Changed: Perform an analysis of your strengths, weaknesses, opportunities, and threats.

Exercise 8: Document Your Vision's Purpose and Value: Equip yourself to communicate why your vision should be believed and supported.

Exercise 9: Create Your Own Recipe for Clarity: Create the equation for clarity and success.

Are you ready to reignite the desire to win and do more than expected? Are you ready to build your Clarity Blueprint? To see how you can better succeed at the speed of life, perform the following exercises.

Exercise 1: Create Voluntary Change

The willingness to change plays a huge role in your ability to succeed. Voluntary change, which does not require anyone to push you or mandate that you do new things, is the kind of change you should seek. To enable smooth, low-stress change, you need to become aware of what you can *and should* change.

Change Audit

Consider, then document on the following template:

1. What opportunities and choices present themselves to you daily?
2. What causes you to feel stressed or rushed?
3. What are the five most important actions you take that bring value to your business or personal life?
4. What are five actions you can either delegate or spend less time on?
5. If you spent less time on the actions in #4 and focused more on the actions in #3, what would that mean to your effectiveness?

Change Audit

1. My daily opportunities and choices:	
2. My stressors:	
3. Top 5 most important actions that bring value to my business or personal life:	1. 2. 3. 4. 5.
4. Top 5 actions I can either delegate or spend less time on:	1. 2. 3. 4. 5.
5. If I spent less time on the actions in #4 and focused more on the actions in #3, that would mean:	

Change Audit: Example

1. **My daily opportunities and choices:**	*1. What to put in my daily schedule* *2. Family/personal vs. business time spent* *3. Time for personal development*
2. **My stressors:**	*1. Planning meetings—chasing down individuals and finding common time* *2. Interruptions when I am working* *3. Badly planned, time-wasting meetings and conference calls*
3. **Top 5 most important actions that bring value to my business or personal life:**	*1. Following up regularly with potential clients until they become actual clients* *2. Exceeding my clients' expectations, which creates long-lasting client relationships* *3. Continuing to develop my skills and offerings* *4. Balancing work and family life* *5. Creating and sticking to a schedule*
4. **Top 5 actions I can either delegate or spend less time on:**	*1. Planning meetings* *2. Creating agendas* *3. Recovering from interruptions* *4. Wasting time on nonessential activities* *5. Staying up late to finish noncritical projects*
5. **If I spent less time on the actions in #4 and focused more on the actions in #3, that would mean:**	*More time to: follow up with clients, spend time on personal development, and increase family time. Less stress from wasted time or inefficient meetings. Increased revenue.*

Exercise 2: Understand Your Influences

You make all decisions based on your personal belief window, which frames all your views of people, places, and things, and influences the action you take regarding those same people, places, and things. Some of these beliefs may be erroneous, and this exercise will help you understand why you accept or reject ideas and people, and eliminate false beliefs.

Your Belief Window

1. First, consider this: How would an erroneous framing of an event, idea, or person impact your results?
2. Second, document your beliefs (what you believe to be true, false, correct, incorrect, appropriate, inappropriate, possible, and impossible) using the following template:

My Belief Window

1. Self	
2. Work	
3. Family	
4. Love	
5. Enemies	
6. Friends	
7. Spirituality	
8. Recreation	
9. Politics	
10. Money	

My Belief Window: Example

1. Self	*I am a strong professional with a good work ethic and integrity. I am also a devoted parent and spouse who makes time for his family.*
2. Work	*My work is very important to me, but not so important that I would sacrifice integrity or family time pursuing my career.*
3. Family	*Family is the most important aspect of my life, and everything I do reflects on my drive to support and nurture them.*
4. Love	*My relationship with my spouse takes work, and I am committed to improving our communication and daily interaction.*
5. Enemies	*Inevitably, people will dislike me, but I will be a good and ethical person who does not burn bridges.*
6. Friends	*I am not a highly social person; my time and effort go first to family and second to my career.*
7. Spirituality	*Pleasing and serving God is the pinnacle of my motivators.*
8. Recreation	*Time must be set aside to be spent in pleasurable ways, but not at the expense of career, and preferably not in overly selfish methods.*
9. Politics	*I am up to date on current politics and what shapes my community, and I work to elect individuals who uphold my priorities.*
10. Money	*Money can be trouble, and it can be a blessing. I work to enable myself and my family to have enough money to satisfy our needs and wants; however, it is not my overall motivator.*

Exercise 3: Understand Your Strategic Beliefs

If you feel that there is not enough time to do all you have to do or that the results you are experiencing are less than you want or expect, you probably need to adjust one or more of your strategic beliefs. This is a polite way of saying that you need to develop a new way of thinking about what it takes to really be successful in your professional and personal life. You believe some things to be true that are not true, and the probable cause is a lack of clarity.

Strategic Belief Adjustment

1. After reviewing your belief window (Exercise 2), consider whether anything you listed may not actually be true.
2. Repeat #1, but approach your consideration as if it were ten years ago.
3. Think about the differences, and consider that in ten years, today's answers may be just as dissimilar.

Exercise 4: Outline What You Need to Do to Get What You Want

Taking small steps is the true basis of achievement. Dividing a large goal into manageable tasks increases your chances for success. For most of us, "overnight" success results from taking lots of small steps that are connected to our dream.

Action Plan

Using the following template:

1. Document your overarching goal or objective.
2. List the tasks and actions necessary to reach that objective, providing deadlines and names of people necessary to help.

Action Plan

Goal or Objective:			
Tasks		**Who**	**When**
1.			
2.			
3.			
4.			
5.			
6.			
7.			
8.			
9.			
10.			

Action Plan: Example

Goal or Objective:	*Start my own consulting business and bring in revenue in excess of $100,000 in the first year of operation*		
Tasks		**Who**	**When**
1. Develop business plan		*Self*	*Sept. 30*
2. Find investors or capital		*Self*	*Oct. 15*
3. Develop marketing, financial, branding plans		*Self*	*Oct. 30*
4. Determine strategic partnerships		*Self*	*Oct. 30*
5. Begin building client list		*Self*	*Nov. 1*
6. Hire sales and marketing team		*Self*	*Nov. 1*
7. Generate at least two leads a week		*Sales person*	*Nov. 15*
8. Upgrade Web site and improve online marketing presence		*Marketing team*	*Nov. 15*
9. Leverage strategic partnerships—share e-mail lists, etc.		*Marketing team*	*Nov. 30*
10. Write book		*Self*	*Dec. 1*

Exercise 5: Document Your Vision

You are successful when you achieve objectives or goals you establish in advance. If you have no vision, there is nothing to tie your objectives to and nothing to help you measure your performance or progress. So a vision not only becomes something to *motivate* you and to provide the *power* to change your behavior, it also becomes the plumb line or *measuring stick* that helps you keep everything together as you execute your plans. A clear vision opens up opportunities and connections and empowers you to better make strategic choices to get superior results.

Vision Creation

Using the following template, consider and document:

1. What do you really want, personally or professionally?
2. Why do you want it?

My Vision

1. What I want:	
2. Why I want it:	

My Vision: Example

1. What I want:	*Start my own consulting business and bring in revenue greater than $100,000 in the first year of operation*
2. Why I want it:	*It will improve my financial situation*

Exercise 6: Unlock Your Internal Keys to Success

Authentic vision will be most frequently discovered or birthed from your own personal experience, strengths, and gifts. Every human being can lay claim to something he or she has that no other person has—and that includes you. Whereas many lives may exhibit some common experiences and characteristics, the *unique* experiences of your life belong to you and you alone. Within those unique experiences, your gifts and talents are exposed, and knowing what those gifts and talents are will increase your effectiveness and value.

Your Strengths and Gifts

Using the following template, consider and document:

1. What characteristics describe you?
2. What characteristics do *not* describe you?
3. What are your roles?
4. What are your top priorities?
5. How do others perceive you?
6. What do others misunderstand about you?

My Strengths & Gifts

1. Characteristics that describe me:	
2. Characteristics that do not describe me:	
3. My roles:	
4. My top priorities:	
5. How others perceive me:	
6. What others misunderstand about me:	

My Strengths & Gifts: Example

1. **Characteristics that describe me:**	*Ethical, professional, cultured, kind, devoted, disciplined, easygoing, intelligent*
2. **Characteristics that do not describe me:**	*Prejudiced, small-minded, unkind, selfish, unethical, lazy*
3. **My roles:**	*Professional, parent, spouse, child, volunteer, mentor*
4. **My top priorities:**	*1. Further my career to enable me to provide for my family* *2. Develop good, long-lasting relationships with my loved ones* *3. Volunteer and give charitably*
5. **How others perceive me:**	*Disciplined, "nose to the grindstone," driven, busy, successful*
6. **What others misunderstand about me:**	*I am very devoted to my family and put them above everything*

Exercise 7: Explore Where You Are Today, Why You Might Not Be Going Where You Want, and What Can Be Changed

Many people believe they have clarity when they have produced goals and have worked out the necessary action steps. These tools are important, but they are more directly related to your ability to focus and keep that focus on the main things. There are two points that must be factually known to produce clarity:

1. Where you want to be when your vision becomes reality
2. An objective understanding of current conditions

These two points must be described in words that can be easily understood, and they must be wrapped with understanding the "why." You must understand why you want to go where you want to go, and you must understand why you are where you are today. Analyzing your strengths, weaknesses, opportunities, and threats increases your ability to focus and keep that focus on the main things.

SWOT Analysis

Using the following template, document your:

1. Strengths (top tools to leverage)
2. Weaknesses (areas to improve or change)
3. Opportunities (roadblocks, both real-world and self-imposed, to overcome)
4. Threats (reasons why you might fail)

SWOT Analysis

1. Strengths:	
2. Weaknesses:	
3. Opportunities:	
4. Threats:	

SWOT Analysis: Example

1. Strengths:	*Educated, intelligent, good connections, excellent team/organization, healthy family, supportive spouse, strong business, satisfied clients, upward growth curve*
2. Weaknesses:	*Time management, not delegating as much or as well as I should, propensity to procrastinate, occasionally irritable with staff and family*
3. Opportunities:	*Delegate more, hire an assistant, make more time for self and family, create daily to-do lists, strategically partner with others who can help build my business*
4. Threats:	*Strong competition, unstable economy, keeping staff motivated and loyal, spending quality time with family before kids have grown*

Exercise 8: Document Your Vision's Purpose and Value

A vision without a clear purpose and strong value may be perceived as whimsical and unbelievable. Therefore, you must concisely define your vision's purpose and value and communicate that purpose and value to all involved to create buy-in and reach the desired results. Defining your vision permits you to better communicate why your vision should be believed and supported.

Purpose and Value Definition

Refer back to your vision (Exercise 5). Using the following template, consider and document:

1. Why is your vision important to you?
2. Why is the success of your vision important to others?

My Vision's Purpose and Value

1. Why my vision is important to me:	
2. Why the success of my vision is important to others:	

My Vision's Purpose and Value: Example

1. Why my vision is important to me:	*My vision is important to me because it will create long-term financial security for me.*
2. Why the success of my vision is important to others:	*My financial security and success directly affect my family and employees.*

Exercise 9: Create Your Own Recipe for Clarity

The basic definition of clarity: having an unfettered view of your vision, which is what you want and why you want it, fed by an understanding of its purpose and value. When people understand the why of things (i.e., the purpose and value), the combination produces a level of clarity that has enough influence to actually become motivational. It becomes the fuel of voluntary change and enables you to be pulled toward your vision, rather than pushed.

$$\frac{\text{what} + \text{why}}{\text{purpose} + \text{value}} = \text{clarity}$$

The Clarity Equation

Your Clarity Equation

Using your answers from Exercises 5 and 8 (your vision and its purpose and value), create your own Clarity Equation on the following template. Document what you really want, personally and professionally, why you want it, why it's important to you, and why your success is important to others.

My Clarity Equation

What:	+	Why:
Purpose:	+	Value:

My Clarity Equation: Example

What: *Start my own consulting business and bring in revenue in excess of $100,000 in the first year of operation.*	+	Why: *It will improve my financial situation.*
Purpose: *It will create long-term financial security for me.*	+	Value: *My financial security and success directly affect my family and employees.*

Now that you've created your Clarity Blueprint, you're ready for the next set of exercises, which will help you develop your Focus Blueprint. Knowing how and on what to focus is the second step of implementing Strategic Acceleration, and that sets you up to successfully execute your vision.

APPENDIX B

Creating Your Focus Blueprint

☞ *You need to develop habits to fully focus and produce long-term success.*

In Appendix A, you developed your Clarity Blueprint to help you get real insight into your vision. You should now have a pretty good idea of all of the following:

- *What* you really want
- *Why* you want it
- *How to capitalize* on your positive aspects and maximize your effectiveness
- *What needs to change* in order for you to be more successful

You are clear about the path you'll be taking, and you understand all the reasons why you're setting off down that road. You have true clarity and are ready for the next step: *developing focus.*

Clarity and focus are so closely related, you might think they are almost the same. However, clarity *precedes* focus, and clarity plays a major role in making focus possible. When you are clear about what you want—and about the value of what you want to do—that gives you the ability to identify the high-leverage activities that most deserve your time. In that sense, clarity is the foundation on which focus is established. Although both clarity and focus are strategic in nature, they are different:

- Clarity is a *strategic condition* that empowers you to clearly see where you want to go.
- Focus is a *strategic skill* that you must learn to enable you to stay on track, persevere, and finish well.

Creating Your Focus Blueprint

So what's the next step in implementing Strategic Acceleration? Creating your Focus Blueprint (templates for which can be downloaded at www.tonyjeary.com), which will help you develop that strategic skill and succeed. The Focus Blueprint is a detailed plan that outlines everything you'll need to concentrate on as you pursue your vision and advance your strategic goals and objectives. In this section, you'll use four exercises to learn how to critically examine both where you want to go and where you *really* are today, identify high-leverage activities, eliminate distractions, and ultimately develop insight and habits that will change your life:

Exercise 10: Evaluate Your Current Focus Skills: Keep a two-week journal to determine where you are today.

Exercise 11: Improve Your Focus Skills: Review the journal and see what improvements you can make.

Exercise 12: Get Clear on Current Conditions: Understand your strategic positives and strategic negatives.

Exercise 13: Develop Your Strategic Plan: Document what you want and how you'll do it, ensuring you're focused on high-leverage activities.

▪ ▪ ▪

After you work through these exercises, you will start the last phase of implementing Strategic Acceleration. In Appendix C, you'll develop your Execution Blueprint, or a set of tools to help you create buy-in, leverage the skills and expertise of others, and ultimately realize the holistic success of your vision.

Exercise 10: Evaluate Your Current Focus Skills

Determining your need for focus initially involves understanding what focus is and how it can be jeopardized. It also involves understanding how well—or how poorly—you currently focus.

Two-Week Focus Journal

Write down your priorities for each day and the specific things you intend to *finish* each day. Then keep an activity log of all that happens to you during the day. Be particularly mindful to log each distraction you experience and the amount of time you invested in the distraction. If you keep this log faithfully for two weeks, you will have a clear picture of what is going on in your life each day concerning focus.

Following is a sample template to use in your own journal. Then an example is provided after the template to help you plan and examine your own day.

Two-Week Focus Journal

Date:	
Today's Priorities:	1. 2. 3. 4. 5.
Today's Tasks:	1. 2. 3. 4. 5.

Activity/Distraction Log:		Description	Time Spent
Time:			

Two-Week Focus Journal: Example

Date:		*July 17, 2008*	
Today's Priorities:		1. *Begin to improve Web site* 2. *Get more business* 3. *Understand current financial situation*	
Today's Tasks:		1. *Work with Web designer on templates* 2. *Develop updated Web copy* 3. *Follow up with leads from last week* 4. *Cold call at least five new prospects* 5. *Review ledger with bookkeeper*	
Activity/Distraction Log:		Description	Time Spent
Time:	8:00 a.m.	*Phone call with Web designer*	.75
	9:00 a.m.	*Began drafting landing page copy*	.25
	9:30 a.m.	*Voice mail to two leads*	.25
	10:00 a.m.	*Return phone call from lead*	.50
	10:30 a.m.	*Voice mail to two new prospects*	.25
	10:45 a.m.	*Unscheduled phone call from supplier*	.50
	1:00 p.m.	*Unscheduled visit from Mark in HR*	.25
	1:30 p.m.	*Phone call from prospect*	.50
	2:30 p.m.	*Unscheduled phone call from VP*	1.00
	3:30 p.m.	*Unscheduled visit from Nan*	.25
	3:45 p.m.	*Meeting with bookkeeper*	2.00
	6:00 p.m.	*Drove home; encountered traffic*	1.50
	8:00 p.m.	*Continued on Web site copy*	.50

Exercise 11: Improve Your Focus Skills

Now that you've completed your two-week Focus Journal, you should have a clear picture of how well you currently focus. You also are positioned to make an informed choice about making a commitment to improve.

Journal Evaluation

When you complete your Focus Journal, look for how many minutes each day you lose to distractions that barge into your mind and lead you on unplanned activities. Specifically, take a closer look at the priorities you established for each day and the specific things you intended to *finish* each day. Make a list of the priorities and tasks you did not complete on the day in question, and then subject each of them to a couple of tough questions. Ask yourself:

- Why didn't I complete the work I had prioritized to complete each day?
- What happened that caused me not to complete them?

Four strategic facts and characteristics about your behavior confirm your ability to execute and focus at a higher level:

1. Fewer distractions
2. More high-leverage activities
3. On-time performance
4. Increased productivity

Do you see any improvement in those areas?

Exercise 12: Get Clear on Current Conditions

There are two critical categories of information that must be collected to produce clarity concerning your current condition: strategic positives and strategic negatives.

Strategic Positives

Strategic positives are the strengths you possess that most powerfully impact your ability to succeed. There are five questions to ask that will help you identify those strengths, listed in the following questionnaire.

My Strategic Positives

Question	Definition	Your Answer
1. What is my competitive advantage?	Things that make your offering unique and determine market share and overall success	
2. What has made me great?	Things that have produced the foundation for your current success	
3. How do my customers and associates view me?	How your customers and employees view you as well as the value they receive from your offering, and why they buy it	
4. What are the top three facts that determine my ability to win?	Two or three core strategic principles that drive success over a long period of time	
5. What strategic opportunities exist that I should pursue?	How you can add value to your product or service or create new opportunities	

My Strategic Positives: Example

Question	Definition	Your Answer
1. What is my competitive advantage?	Things that make your offering unique and determine market share and overall success	• *Great reputation* • *Strong brand presence* • *High-quality product* • *Proprietary process*
2. What has made me great?	Things that have produced the foundation for your current success	• *Work ethic* • *Talented staff* • *Unique product offering* • *Strong marketing resources*
3. How do my customers and associates view me?	How your customers and employees view you as well as the value they receive from your offering, and why they buy it	• *Low prices* • *Recognizable brand* • *Great service* • *Good value for the money*
4. What are the top three facts that determine my ability to win?	Two or three core strategic principles that drive success over a long period of time	• *Always provide value that exceeds my customers' expectations* • *Complete tasks and projects ahead of schedule* • *Create and sustain a highly consistent brand that reflects the value my customers will receive*
5. What strategic opportunities exist that I should pursue?	How you can add value to your product or service or create new opportunities	• *Turning negatives into positives* • *Better meeting customers' needs* • *Setting and meeting more aggressive deadlines*

Strategic Negatives

Strategic negatives are the factors that most powerfully contribute to failure or less-than-satisfactory results. The four questions listed in the following questionnaire will help you identify those negatives.

My Strategic Negatives

Question	Definition	Your Answer
1. What internal complaints have historically created challenges and affected the satisfaction of my employees?	Consistent complaints that come from within	
2. What are my top three customer complaints?	Consistent complaints that come from the outside	
3. What do my competitors believe to be my strategic shortcomings?	What competitors are saying about your potential strategic weaknesses	
4. What are the top three factors that can cause me to lose?	Issues that consistently contribute to your failures	

My Strategic Negatives: Example

Question	Definition	Your Answer
1. What internal complaints have historically created challenges and affected the satisfaction of my employees?	Consistent complaints that come from within	• *Too many meetings* • *Overwhelming workloads* • *Minimal advertising budget* • *Draconian management*
2. What are my top three customer complaints?	Consistent complaints that come from the outside	• *Poor reliability* • *High price* • *Lack of positive customer-service experiences*
3. What do my competitors believe to be my strategic shortcomings?	What competitors are saying about your potential strategic weaknesses	• *Unstable management* • *Saturated market* • *Poor value for product quality*
4. What are the top three factors that can cause me to lose?	Issues that consistently contribute to your failures	• *High price* • *Inability to communicate value* • *Inability to effectively communicate selling position*

Exercise 13: Develop Your Strategic Plan

In an ideal strategic plan, three tiers of focus support execution of the vision, and they collectively produce the power to propel you across the gap to success. This exercise will help you define and document the following:

Strategies

At Tier 1 are the strategies you must develop to execute your vision successfully. Strategies represent what you must *become* along the way as you cross the gap to your vision. Strategies are about creating conditions that produce unique, competitive advantages that come together to successfully execute your vision. Strategies should relate to *value creation* and *value enhancement* because that is what creates long-term sustainability of your competitive advantage and your success. For that reason, creating relevant strategies is the most significant critical success factor in being able to identify your high-leverage activities.

Objectives

On Tier 2 are objectives that lead to successfully executing your strategies. These goals are more tactical in nature. The most important thing to remember about creating Tier 2 objectives is that they must be based on the strategies you created in Tier 1. Objectives are specific components of what your strategy must achieve, and they represent the goals that are most critical to your achieving those strategies. When you begin to establish your objectives, you are beginning to transition into focusing on the action(s) you need to take in the present. In contrast, the strategies created in Tier 1 have more of a *long-term perspective* and represent how far you can see. The objectives you create to achieve those strategies represent the more *immediate tasks* you must perform so you can actually go as far as you can see.

Actions

Finally, at Tier 3, you see the actions or specific steps that must be accomplished for you to successfully reach your objectives. Action steps are mini-objectives made up of the *specific things you must do on a daily and weekly basis.* Action steps are the most immediate issues you must deal with and they are always found in the near present. Consider if the action step will have a direct impact on helping you successfully complete the objective to which the action step is related.

Following is a blank template you can use to start developing your own strategic plan. Remember that a vision can have more than one strategy, and a strategy can have more than one objective. This template keeps it simple, but you can expand it easily to suit your vision's specific requirements. After this template is an example to help you populate your own plan.

Strategic Plan

Vision:	
Tier 1—Strategies	
Tier 2—Objectives	
Tier 3—Actions	

Strategic Plan: Example

Vision: *Improve my overall financial situation by increasing salary*	
Tier 1—Strategies	*Advance career; get a raise*
Tier 2—Objectives	*Get promoted to the next level of management*
Tier 3—Actions	*Meet with supervisor to discuss my strengths and weaknesses (determine current landscape)*
	Determine what I need to do to move up on the corporate ladder (training, finding replacement, etc.)
	Set milestones with manager about proving I am ready for the next level of responsibility
	Pursue milestones as set forth by manager
	Meet with manager to review training and other milestones and discuss actual promotion

Creating Your Execution Blueprint

☞ *Executing your vision means combining all of your clarity and focus to strategically communicate and achieve results.*

A s you know, clarity empowers you to clearly see where you want to go, and focus enables you to stay on track, persevere, and finish well. In Appendix A, you created your Clarity Blueprint to help you define your vision, why you are pursuing it, how to make the most out of your strengths, and what to alter to ensure you're operating to the best of your ability. Appendix B helped you develop your Focus Blueprint to show you *where* you are today with your focus skills, what needs to be improved, and on what you need to concentrate. You're now ready for the last step of the Strategic Acceleration process: *execution*, which is the act of combining all of your clarity and focus to strategically communicate, exceed expectations, and ultimately realize your vision.

The six exercises in this appendix (with templates available at www.tonyjeary.com) will help you develop skills that will enable you to fully execute your vision:

Exercise 14: Determine What to Say and How to Say It: Learn the 3-D Outline technique to help you deliver each and every presentation with maximum impact.

Exercise 15: Give Value and Do More than Is Expected: Determine how you can exceed others' expectations, and provide unexpected value to them.

Exercise 16: Document What Is and Is Not Working Well: Identify the things you do that produce the greatest impact, as well as what may actually reduce your overall effectiveness.

Exercise 17: Describe Your Hope and Great Goal for the Future: Create a vision statement that articulates the future as fact and will give others clarity about your vision.

Exercise 18: Examine the Behaviors You Most Value: Document what is most important to you so that others understand your priorities.

Exercise 19: Understand What You Are and What You Want to Be: Create the statements that form your images of influence that transmit strategic presence.

■ ■ ■

After you've created your Execution Blueprint, you're ready to merge it with your Clarity and Focus Blueprints. Review them frequently to ensure you're still clear, focused, and executing with impact. Your vision may change, its purpose and value may change, your high-leverage activities may change, and most important, *you* may change. In fact, I hope that learning the Strategic Acceleration process will be a catalyst for tremendous changes in how you view yourself, move through the world, lead, and pursue your vision. These blueprints form the map to guide and make sure you're on track, growing, and reaping the real results you want.

I welcome your feedback and progress reports; please drop me a line at tonyj@tonyjeary.com and let me know how this book has helped you succeed at the speed of life. Let me know how I or my team can further help you and/or your organization. We love results and helping people win. Much success!

Exercise 14: Determine What to Say and How to Say It

Effective communication strategy requires you to plan *what* you want to say and how you will *deliver* the message. As you know, successfully executing your vision depends on how effectively you can persuade others to help you. You may need to explain your vision and its importance to a family member, to a group of investors, to a whole organization, or to your team. An effective delivery will enable you to convince others to take action on your behalf. This exercise will teach you the 3-D Outline process, which describes *what* you want to say, *why* you should say it, and of course *how* you'll say it. It outlines all of the actions behind a successful delivery.

3-D Outline

This matrix will help you organize your thoughts and actions by giving you space to document information about your audience, objectives, key points, timing, and more. After you use it a few times, you'll see how you can customize it to fit your unique presentation needs. Whether you're presenting to one person or a large group, the 3-D Outline enables you to keep everything you need on track and in line.

3-D Outline™

Presentation Title:				Delivery Date:	
Audience:				Start Time:	
Objectives:				End Time:	
Final Preparation:	☐		☐		
	☐		☐		

#	Start Time	Length	What	Why	How	Who
1.						
2.						
3.						
4.						
5.						
6.						
7.						
8.						
9.						
10.						

3-D Outline™: Example

Presentation Title:	Moving Forward: The New Team Vision		Delivery Date:	08/08
Audience:	Directors, managers, administrative staff, interns		Start Time:	9:00 a.m.
Objectives:	• Explain the new vision • create buy-in and commitment	• Describe Responsibilities • Excite and Inspire	End Time:	10:00 a.m.
Final Preparation:	[] Print materials		[] Create vision video with group leaders	
	[] Arrange for large conference room		[]	

#	Start Time	Length	What	Why	How	Who
1.	9:00 a.m.	15	Opening: purpose, process, payoff	Describe objectives, agenda, benefits	Stand up	Kyle
2.	9:15 a.m.	15	Vision video	Create excitement	Video	
3.	9:30 a.m.	15	Vision description	Explain new goals, purpose, value, etc.	Stand up, slides	Kyle
4.	9:45 a.m.	30	What this means for you	Share what to expect, changes, new responsibilities	Stand up, slides	Kyle
5.	10:15 a.m.	30	Concerns & questions	Address concerns	Roundtable discussion	Kyle, directors
6.	10:45 a.m.	10	How we'll do it	Determine goals by team	Small-group activity	Directors, admin staff, interns
7.	10:55 a.m.	5	Conclusion	Wrap up the day	Stand up	Kyle
8.						
9.						
10.		2 hours				

Exercise 15: Give Value and Do More than Is Expected

My father taught the most important business principle of my life: "Give value; do more than is expected!" For individuals and businesses to realize their vision and truly succeed, this principle should drive all thought processes.

Exceeding Expectations

This exercise will help you determine how you can exceed others' expectations and provide unexpected value to them. You'll be asked to consider and document your top talents and skills, your loves and passions, your uniquenesses and value, and how you could better leverage all of them. Finally, you'll write a "fantasy testimonial," which is what you'd like a raving fan to say about you. At the end of the exercise, you'll see how you can better capitalize on what makes you *you*, which will in turn enable you to give value and do more than is expected.

Exceeding Expectations

Question	Your Answer
What are your top talents and skills?	
What do you love to do?	
What are you passionate about?	
What truly makes you unique?	
What do others value about you?	
What could you do to better highlight or leverage the above?	
Write your "fantasy testimonial"—what you'd like a raving fan to say about you.	

Exceeding Expectations: Example

Question	Your Answer
What are your top talents and skills?	*Presenting, inspiring others, setting positive examples for the team, time management, mentoring*
What do you love to do?	*Help others grow, inspire others to change positively, speak and train*
What are you passionate about?	*Growth, change, being positive*
What truly makes you unique?	*People really do listen when I speak; they seem to readily engage with me and what I have to say*
What do others value about you?	*Honesty, integrity, authentic "self," obvious commitment to the team, work ethic*
What could you do to better highlight or leverage the above?	*Talk more about why my values are important to me, show others how to be more effective through more mentorship and one-on-one training/interaction*
Write your "fantasy testimonial"—what you'd like a raving fan to say about you.	*"Carolyn is by far the most nurturing and positive leader I've ever had. She always takes the time to listen and guide me, and she has really helped me grow both personally and professionally. Through her mentorship, she's taught me the skills I need to mentor others, and as a result, our team is much more connected and growth-oriented than ever before."*

Exercise 16: Document What Is and Is Not Working Well

Here, you'll identify the things you do that produce the greatest impact, as well as what may actually reduce your overall effectiveness.

More Of/Less Of (MOLO) Matrix

The MOLO Matrix will allow you to see what you need to keep doing as you pursue your vision, as well as what you need to change to be more effective. From there, you'll see the high-leverage activities that deserve the majority of your time and effort. Focusing on those actions will help you move the results needle.

MOLO Matrix

What Do I Need To ...	Actions	Why
. . . Do More Of?		
. . . Do Less Of?		
. . . Start Doing?		
. . . Stop Doing?		

MOLO Matrix: Example

What Do I Need To . . .	Actions	Why
. . . Do More Of?	Communicating with my team about project status	Keeps everyone on track and aligned
	Holding regular team-building events	Creates team synergy
	Delegating admin. tasks to my assistant	Frees up my time for other actions
	Creating daily to-do and priority lists	Organizes my day
	Reviewing my Focus Journal	Keeps me focused
. . . Do Less Of?	Taking on tasks of others	Sucks away my time
	Worrying about status of others' projects	Eats up attention and focus
	Procrastinating on financials	Makes more work for the team
	Staying at work excessively late	Sets a bad example for the team
	Letting others run my meetings	Diminishes control I need in this project
. . . Start Doing?	Mentoring others	Builds skills, brings pleasure
	Eating lunch every day	Keeps up my strength
	Reviewing my blueprints	Keeps me on track
	Encouraging my staff to keep Focus Journals	Increases overall effectiveness
	Creating detailed agendas for each meeting	Saves time and creates better results
. . . Stop Doing?	Worrying	Nothing good comes of it
	Micromanaging	Creates resentment
	Showing up late for meetings	Sets a bad example
	Checking BlackBerry constantly	Decreases focus
	Working every weekend	Impacts quality of life

Images of Influence

As discussed in Chapter 8, the images of influence you create are shaped by all the things others see about you. They are shaped in many ways, but three strategic building blocks are most important:

1. Your vision statement
2. Your behavioral priorities
3. Your presence statements/characteristics

The following three exercises will help you create those three building blocks, ensuring that you have congruent and authentic images of influence.

Exercise 17: Describe Your Hope and Great Goal for the Future

A vision statement expresses your hope and the great goal you have for the future. A vision statement is a specific statement that articulates the future as fact and will give others clarity about your vision.

Vision Statement

As you go about creating your vision statement, you should consider what you want, why you want it, and what positive things will happen when your vision is executed.

My Vision Statement

My vision is:

My Vision Statement: Example

My vision is: *to be a strong, strategic asset to my team by continuously focusing on giving great value and modeling great leadership. This will continue to build my legacy and be an inspiration for those I lead.*

Exercise 18: Examine the Behaviors You Most Value

There are behaviors you most value and expect in yourself and others. When people understand what is most important to you, they understand your priorities and what matters most to you concerning their own behavior.

Behavioral Priorities

Here you'll list the behaviors you most value, which will enable you to communicate their importance to others and demonstrate those same skills in your own everyday activities.

My Behavioral Priorities

Behavioral Priority	Why It's Important	How I Demonstrate It

My Behavioral Priorities: Example

Behavioral Priority	Why It's Important	How I Demonstrate It
Being committed to family	All of my personal decisions are driven by how they will benefit my loved ones	Thinking through impacts, benefits, etc., asking questions, being empathetic
Knowing how to ask good questions	Gathers vital information from others	Preparing questions and being thoughtful during answers
Being a good listener	Indicates focus and care	Fully focusing on the speaker—no phone, BlackBerry, etc.—and taking notes
Having a good work ethic	Ensures productivity and sets a good example	Showing up on time, working hard, exhibiting professional behaviors that feed focus and execution
Serving as a strong leader	A good leader supports a good team	Mentoring, listening, taking management classes, being professional

Exercise 19: Understand What You Are and What You Want to Be

It is important to understand what you are and what you want to be. It's equally important to know what you're *not* and what you do not want to be! You should not just determine the answers to these questions. You need to teach them, talk about them, and allow them to be reflected in all you say and do. They become statements that form images of influence that transmit your strategic presence.

Presence Statements

Think through what you value most in yourself and in others. Think about what you want others to see in you and to emulate. Think about the other side, too—what are you *not*?

My Presence Statements

I am:	• • •
I do not:	• • •

My Presence Statements: Example

I am:	• *Disciplined and hardworking* • *Empathetic and sensitive to others' needs* • *Deadline-driven and team-oriented*
I do not:	• *Procrastinate and give others the bulk of the burden* • *Pursue my agenda and goals without concern for others* • *Show up late or miss deadlines*

GLOSSARY

Actions: Specific steps that must be accomplished to success-fully reach your objectives.

Behavioral priorities: Priorities that address the behaviors you most value and expect in yourself and others. When people understand what is most important to you, they understand your priorities and what matters most to you concerning their own behaviors and actions.

Belief window: The way in which you view the world, your role in that world, and the relationships you have with everybody in it. It contains everything you believe to be true, false, correct, incorrect, appropriate, inappropriate, possible, and impossible. It frames all of your views of people, places, and things, and creates the perceptions and feelings you have about everything. It influences the actions you take regarding those same people, places, and things. It determines all of your choices and actions, and it allows information you consider important to enter your mind and be retained. It also blocks out what you do not consider important and screens information and circumstances you don't think you need.

Clarity: Understanding clearly your targets and the "why" behind reaching them (personally and professionally). It can also be described as having an unfettered view of your vision, which is what you want and why you want it, fed by an understanding of its purpose and value.

Clarity Blueprint: A plan that includes what you want to do, why you want to do it, how you will do it, the benefit of doing it, and the negative result of not doing it.

Clarity effect: The power of a clear vision that provides the ability to see and pursue necessary actions.

Clarity Equation: Your vision, what you want, and why you want it, powered by its purpose and value, equal clarity.

Comfort zones: A mental state in which you have lost the momentum to pursue your vision because you have accepted where you are as the best you need to be or do.

Competitive advantage: The factors that make you or your company or your products or services unique and that impact your market share and overall success. The available resources and your organizational capabilities combine to form your (or your organization's, or your business's) distinctive competencies.

Competitive opinion: What your competitors believe are your strategic shortcomings.

Current conditions: Your vision of where you want to be as compared to the reality of where you are. High-leverage activities are discovered in the gap between the two.

Distraction: The opposite of focus. It happens whenever you allow something to enter your mind that takes you away from doing what you should be doing. It is the path of least resistance because the most natural activity for your mind is to take in information.

Effectiveness Ladder: Four specific steps to become more effective at what you do. Rung #1: Become Aware of the Need: You become aware of something you cannot do. Rung #2: Clarify the Need: You become aware of what you did not know. However, you still can't do whatever it is you did not know how to do. Rung #3: Focus on the Need: You embrace the need you have discovered, and you will begin to take the action to respond to it. Rung #4: Execute the Need: The task in question becomes second nature to you, and you can effectively execute and deploy the skills you have learned.

Exceeding expectations: Creating positive experiences that people do not anticipate. Giving value and doing more than is expected.

Execution: The act of combining all of your clarity and focus to strategically communicate, take action, exceed expectations, and ultimately realize your vision.

Failure factors: The top issues that could cause you to lose whatever it is you're working for.

Felt needs: The feeling that something new is needed to provide solutions you can actually implement. Long before solutions for significant problems and challenges are discovered, you can describe the problem and attempts you've made to resolve it, but you can't articulate an exact prescription to fix it.

Focus: The ability to concentrate on what really matters and to filter out what doesn't. This is a thinking skill that is acquired as a result of mental discipline.

High-leverage activities: Actions that are most relevant to your strategic agenda, success, and achievement, and most directly impact the results you need and want. The ability to identify and focus on these significant activities is the major factor in improving and accelerating results.

History: What has produced the foundation of your success. Being aware of those historical success factors is important, and you need to evaluate them with respect to current relevance.

If-then thinking: The explanations occasionally created when a plan or strategy goes sour and the results are less than expected; for example, "If I had known this, then I could've/should've/would've done that."

Images of influence: What others see you do, which affects their perceptions, attitudes, and behavior in subtle but powerful ways. The authenticity of these images of influence is vitally important to your success.

More Of/Less Of (MOLO) Matrix: Identifies the things you do that produce the greatest impact, as well as those things that may actually reduce your overall effectiveness.

Negative procrastination: When you avoid doing something based on flimsy excuses. This affects your results in negative ways.

Neutral expectations: A benchmark description of current conditions, or what we perceive to be the status quo.

Objectives: Action statements that define a result category. Note that strong objectives begin with an action word.

Opportunity inventory: Examining and documenting your greatest strengths and weaknesses, the things you really love to do, and what others value most about you.

Organizational energy: The collective sum of the human spark that powers the desire to win, produces creativity, supports persistence, and establishes the foundation for organizational commitment. When organizational energy is degraded or lost, all of these qualities begin to diminish and the ability to achieve superior results becomes less likely.

Positive procrastination: When you legitimately need some "mental percolation" time to gather your thoughts and get clear on what you need to do.

Presence statements and characteristics: What you are and what you want to be, as well as what you're not, and what you do not want to be.

Procrastination foundations: Strategic beliefs that cause you to procrastinate.

Production: Completing tasks and projects in reduced time frames.

Production Before Perfection (PBP): Working in parallel, adjusting the project as you progress, rather than waiting for every aspect of a project to come into perfect, linear alignment (introduced in my book *Success Acceleration,* Riverside, 2002).

Pulling power: The catalyst for voluntary change that comes from being clear about what you really want.

Purpose: Why what you want is important to you and to others. It is a transcendent concept that actually wraps itself around your vision and carries it forward.

Satisfaction: The opinions and beliefs your customers and employees have about you, your offering, and its value.

Speed of life: Fast-paced living and the opportunities, choices, and pressures that present themselves daily, influenced by technology, information access, enhanced communication abilities, and accelerated innovation.

Strategic Acceleration: The ability to expedite change and increase effectiveness more quickly, powered by clarity, engaged with focus, and converted into superior results via execution.

Strategic beliefs: Ways of thinking about what it takes to really be successful in your professional and personal life. The word "strategic" deals with "why" issues, whereas the word "tactical" deals with "how" issues. Therefore, your belief window (the "why" behind your actions and choices) is a set of strategic beliefs.

Strategic impatience: The ability to manage one's patience to ensure that it does not affect execution by becoming procrastination. Instead, it should be used as a tool to motivate you to take action and get things done.

Strategic leverage: The ability to organize your goals and zero in on the activities that produce real results.

Strategic negatives: The factors that most powerfully contribute to failure or less-than-satisfactory results.

Strategic opportunities: Roads that have opened up and become apparent by achieving clarity about your vision; the choices you should pursue that will add value to your product or service, capitalize on your gifts and strengths, and better meet customer needs.

Strategic plan: A plan that organizes your goals in a way that recognizes your specific needs and identifies high-leverage activities. It is topped by the vision, which is supported by strategies, objectives, and actions.

Strategic positives: The strengths you possess that most powerfully impact your ability to succeed.

Strategic presence: The persona that defines the total perception others have about you.

Strategic principles: What drives your business, efforts, and long-term success.

Strategies: Goals that will produce the highest degree of strategic leverage.

Success: Achieving objectives or goals you have established in advance.

Value: Why the success of your vision is important to others. It is an issue of perception of having your expectations not just met, but exceeded.

Vision: What motivates you and provides the power to change your behavior; it is also the plumb line or measuring stick that helps you keep everything together as you execute your plans. It is created by combining opportunity with personal strengths and talents.

Vision creation: The first step toward Strategic Acceleration. Success and getting superior results always begins with vision. A clear vision has the power to consistently produce voluntary change.

Vision statement: An expression of your hope and the great goal you have for the future. A vision statement articulates the future as fact and gives others clarity about your vision.

Voluntary change: The willingness to change proactively, without being pushed by someone else. This type of change plays a huge role in your ability to succeed. It is the key for you to break out of whatever existing conditions you have in your business or personal life that may be holding you back.

About the Author

When many of the world's top executives seek a strategic collaborator, facilitator, and coach, they are eventually led to Tony Jeary. Tony has invested his life and career in helping others discover new clarity for their vision, develop focus on their direction, and create powerful execution strategies that strategically impact achievement and results. Tony's clients include top entrepreneurs, high-achieving corporate leaders, and progressive management teams.

Tony was raised by entrepreneurial parents who thrived on identifying and pursuing new opportunities to serve others. Tony's father taught him the powerful principle that has driven Tony's professional and personal life: "Give value; do more than is expected." Exceeding expectations is the common thread that every Tony Jeary client experiences firsthand.

The development of Tony's Strategic Acceleration Process resulted from his obsession with studying distinctions that characterize top-performing high achievers and organizations. From this study, Tony discovered and proved that the foundational characteristic of great performers was gaining clarity about what they really want and coupling their vision with superior focusing skills and execution strategies.

Tony has been described as a "gifted encourager" who facilitates positive outcomes for others in his role as a strategic collaborator. His list of personal and professional relationships approaches twenty thousand people with whom he connects and nourishes out of his sincere interest in and desire for their success. Tony has personally coached the presidents of organizations including Ford, Wal-Mart, Samsung, EDS, ASTD, New York Life, Firestone, and Sam's Club, to name a few.

Tony has personal experience with both success and failure. He made and lost several million dollars before he was thirty. Today he walks the talk and practices the distinctions that characterize Strategic Acceleration both personally and professionally. He is blessed with a terrific marriage and two great daughters, with whom he has coauthored. He works in the Dallas–Fort Worth area from his private Strategic Acceleration Studio, where scores of top business leaders and executives visit every year.

How We Can Help

Tony Jeary International is a highly specialized firm dedicated to helping individuals and organizations accelerate their results. Our clients are business leaders and entrepreneurs who have a desire to accelerate their performance and enhance their value in the marketplace.

We work with organizations of all sizes and maturity levels that are motivated to improve, grow, and excel. Our primary assignments center on strategic planning and strategic facilitation, based on the methodology outlined in this book.

Tony Jeary is available to address corporate leadership groups and annual meetings, providing unique insight and contagious energy that produces new ways of strategic thinking at every organizational level.

Please call (877) 2 INSPIRE for more information, or visit www.tonyjeary.com for detailed offerings and free resources, and to utilize our unique assessments to quickly evaluate your personal and organizational strategic effectiveness.